Dearest Rosmary,

Good Luck ~

recovery. Remem-

is much #too impo

Take seriously.

Best Regards,

George & Gracie

Malmiee

MIRACLES IN OUR MIDST
Stories of Life, Love, Kindness and Other Miracles

PRESENTED BY
RICHARD L. SCOTT

Written & Compiled
by
Susan Thomas

Published
by
Twyman Towery, Ph.D.
Wessex House Publishing

WESSEX HOUSE PUBLISHING
141 Rue de Grande
Brentwood, Tennessee 37027

Designed by Terry Thornhill
at Big Dot Digital Design

Edited by Ann Betts

Manufactured in the United States of America

Library of Congress Cataloging-in-Publication Data
Miracles in our midst: stories of life, love, kindness
and other miracles/
Richard L. Scott, Susan Thomas and Twyman Towery
96-61487

ISBN: 0-9646872-3-2

DEDICATION

This book is dedicated
to the employees and affiliated physicians
of Columbia. Whether they administer treatment,
deliver food or supplies, perform lab tests,
sweep floors, process accounts, lead teams of co-workers,
or perform other tasks associated with caring for patients
and improving the lives of the people they serve.

All of these individuals have contributed in some way
to the miracles found in these pages.

INTRODUCTION & ACKNOWLEDGMENTS

Each week of the year, I receive countless letters from employees, patients and physicians about "miracles" — from wondrous acts of human kindness to extraordinary medical feats and even seemingly inexplicable spiritual events. All these take place in our lives and around our workplaces, painting a brilliant portrait of life that illuminates acts of gratitude, honesty, compassion, trust, dedication, hope and love. The stories come about because of thousands of individuals who ignore obstacles and give extra encouragement in the day-to-day routine of good, caring people helping one another.

One morning when I was reading another of these many letters, it occurred to me that these remarkable stories are rarely, if ever, seen or heard by anyone beyond the small circle of co-workers, family and friends of those involved. It was then that the concept for this book emerged, driven by the belief that in sharing the stories of everyday heroes in this collection, we could provide many with a place where they could turn for proof positive that miracles of all kinds happen around us, each and every day.

The result of that concept is Miracles In Our Midst, a collection of true stories about real people whose actions bring about those miracles. The stories were shared by members of the Columbia family, and in them they describe events and people through their own experience and perspective, using their words and those of their co-workers. While space prohibited us from using every experience that was shared, my thanks to all who sent in their stories and contributed their hard work to this project. I would particularly like to thank Teresa Yingling Burns and the staff of the National Association of Senior Friends, who helped bring this project to life.

Finally, in keeping with the spirit of this project, proceeds from book sales will help support the National Association of Senior Friends, a group which through its work in support of the needs of senior adults creates its own daily miracles.

Richard L. Scott
Chairman & Chief Executive Officer
Columbia/HCA Healthcare Corporation

CONTENTS

OUT OF THE SHADOWS

The days seemed hotter then, back in the early 1930s in the cotton mill town of Bladenboro, North Carolina. Not even the mighty Atlantic, only 50 miles due east, was strong enough to send a salty ocean breeze over to cool the old wooden porch at Earl Warwick's childhood home.

Earl, now 65, particularly remembers one sizzling summer day when he was a toddler, crawling across the hot planks trying to play — instead discovering something that would rule his life for the next 62 years.

"I crawled right off the end of the porch," Earl says, "and that was the moment, even as young as I was, that I knew I couldn't see. I fell off that porch because I couldn't see where it ended."

Thus began the long odyssey through the shadows that Earl would travel for more than six decades. While his parents — cotton mill workers as most everyone else in the rugged, rural town — loved him, they were at a loss with what to do with a young boy with visual birth defects.

Earl's left eye was totally blind, and the socket around it was noticeably smaller than his right, giving ammunition for other children to taunt him as "one-eye" and worse. His right eye, though normal in size, gave him very limited, shadowy vision, which he could only describe as "always looking through a frosted windshield on a cool morning."

Not knowing what to do, his parents never actively sought treatment or answers for their son's problems, but they did send him to a state school for the blind when he was about eight years old.

"They didn't have any medicine or treatments or anything like that back then," he says. "All they had to help us was warm wash cloths to lay across our eyes when they hurt."

After a half dozen years or so at the school where he learned Braille, Earl left before graduating to return to Bladenboro to tend to his sickly mother. He got a job as a radio operator at the Bladen County Sheriff's Department to support himself and his mother, memorizing the radio dials by touch and conquering the dispatching job with his deep, smooth, authoritative voice.

During those years as a young man, Earl walked or used his thumb to hitch a ride to and from work, as well as make a number of trips to doctors and hospitals in his own search to find out if anything could be done to improve his vision.

"It was the same story wherever I went," he recalls. "They would say they didn't think they could help me but that they would experiment and maybe learn something. After a while, I guess there was a point that I just gave up."

Back in Bladenboro, Earl continued working at the sheriff's department and tending to his mother. In 1965, he married, then his mother died in 1972. Two years later, he retired from his job.

The years went by slowly and quietly after that. The vision in his right eye neither diminished nor improved. If he held something close enough, he could detect particular colors and when he looked up at the sky, he knew if the sun was shining.

In the early 1990s, his wife died. And it was right around that same time that his blind eye began hurting. Looking to ease the discomfort, Earl made an appointment with Shawn F. Riley, M.D., a specialist in diseases of the anterior part of the eye. Earl arranged a ride to the doctor's office, 70 miles away in Supply, North Carolina.

To ease the pain in Earl's blind eye, the doctor recommended a partial prosthesis. Then — out of the blue at least to Earl — Dr. Riley said he believed there was a chance to improve the vision in Earl's right eye.

"I hadn't known Dr. Riley long, but there was something about him that I liked," Earl says. "I trusted him. He didn't want to experiment on me to learn something. He wanted to help me see better."

After countless consultations, tests and talks, a game plan evolved — Earl would require a cornea transplant.

"Dr. Riley told me it was a 50-50 chance that I would be able to see better, and there was only a one-percent chance the operation would take away the little vision that I had," Earl says.

After coming to grips and overcoming the fears he had had as a young man when doctors only wanted to "experiment on me," he told Dr. Riley to "go for it."

Six months later, a suitable donor for a cornea transplant was located, and the surgery began on the morning of October 6, 1994 at Columbia Brunswick Hospital. The necessary surgery was more extensive than originally believed. In the operating room, the doctor discovered that most of the vital components in Earl's eye had grown together, making it necessary for him to "take everything except the retina apart, fix all the parts, then put them back together again, along with the cornea transplant," Earl explains.

It was late in the afternoon before Earl awoke from the surgery. His fingers could feel the shield and dressing strapped across his eye. But when he raised his hand in the air and slowly waved it above his patched eye, he could see the shadows and then the light of the sun beaming through his hospital room window.

The next morning, when the shield and dressing were removed, Earl's vision seemed to be blocked by hundreds of tiny lights flashing before his right eye. But as the hours and then days of recovery passed, the little lights went away, revealing a world Earl had never seen in all of his 62 years.

"It was like dying and going to Heaven," he says. "I was able to look in the mirror and see myself for the very first time. I could see what other people looked like. I could see most everything, including the face of a beautiful little baby. Do you understand what that meant to me? I could really see."

In the two years since his surgery, Earl still marvels over the "vision of life." He has tried, to no avail, to contact the family of the person who unselfishly became an organ donor to offer him a cornea which now allows him "to live and see life" at the same time. Earl also insisted on calling Dr. Riley's mother in Chicago to thank her for having a son who became a doctor who would one day give him sight.

So these days, it doesn't seem quite as hot

when summer falls on Earl's front porch in his home-town of Bladenboro.

While the thermometer may register the same temperature it did years ago, Earl is too busy to notice. Each and every morning, he wakes up eager to get out of bed to see something new — a door-knob, a light switch, a radio or most anything — sim-ple objects to those who have had vision all their lives, yet miracles to a man who as a child could not see the end of his own front porch.

Daphne Yarbrough
Columbia Brunswick Hospital
Supply, North Carolina

HEAVEN SCENT

A cold March wind danced around the dead of night in Dallas as the doctor walked into the small hospital room of Diana Blessing.

Still groggy from surgery, her husband David held her hand as they braced themselves for the latest news. That afternoon of March 10, 1991, complications had forced Diana, only 24-weeks pregnant, to undergo an emergency cesarean to deliver the couple's new daughter, Danae Lu Blessing.

At 12 inches long and weighing only one pound and nine ounces, they already knew she was perilously premature.

Still, the doctor's soft words dropped like bombs.

"I don't think she's going to make it," he said, as kindly as he could. "There's only a 10-percent chance she will live through the night, and even then, if by some slim chance she does make it, her future could be a very cruel one."

Numb with disbelief, David and Diana listened as the doctor described the devastating problems Danae would likely face if she survived. She would never walk. She would never talk. She would probably be blind. She would certainly be prone to other catastrophic conditions from cerebral palsy to complete mental retardation. And on and on.

"No ... No!" was all Diana could say.

She and David, with their 5-year-old son Dustin, had long dreamed of the day they would have a daughter to become a family of four. Now, within a matter of hours, that dream was slipping away.

Through the dark hours of morning as Danae held onto life by the thinnest thread, Diana slipped in and out of drugged sleep, growing more and more determined that their tiny daughter would live — and live to be a healthy, happy young girl. But David, fully awake and listening to additional dire details of their daughter's chances of ever leaving the hospital alive, much less healthy, knew he must confront his wife with the inevitable.

"David walked in and said that we needed to talk about making funeral arrangements," Diana remembers. "I felt so bad for him because he was doing everything, trying to include me in what was going on, but I just wouldn't listen. I couldn't listen.

"I said, 'No, that is not going to happen, no way! I don't care what the doctors say. Danae is not going to die! One day she will be just fine, and she will be coming home with us!' "

As if willed to live by Diana's determination, Danae clung to life hour after hour, with the help of every medical machine and marvel her miniature body could endure. But as those first days passed, a new agony set in for David and Diana.

Because Danae's underdeveloped nervous system was essentially "raw," the lightest kiss or caress only intensified her discomfort — so they couldn't even cradle their tiny baby girl against their chests to offer the strength of their love. All they could do, as Danae struggled alone beneath the ultra-violet light in the tangle of tubes and wires, was to pray that God would stay close to their precious little girl.

There was never a moment when Danae suddenly grew stronger. But as the weeks went by, she did slowly gain an ounce of weight here and an ounce of strength there.

At last, when Danae turned two months old, her parents were able to hold her in their arms for the very first time. And two months later — though doctors continued to gently but grimly warn that her chances of surviving, much less living any kind of normal life, were next to zero — Danae went home from the hospital, just as her mother had predicted.

Today, five years later, Danae is a petite but feisty young girl with glittering gray eyes and a unquenchable zest for life. She shows no signs, whatsoever, of any mental or physical impairments.

Simply, she is everything a little girl can be and more — but that happy ending is far from the end of her story.

One blistering afternoon in the summer of 1996 near her home in Irving, Texas, Danae was sitting in her mother's lap in the bleachers of a local ball park where her brother Dustin's baseball team was practicing. As always, Danae was chattering non-stop with her mother and several other adults sitting nearby when she suddenly fell silent.

Hugging her arms across her chest, Danae asked, "Do you smell that?"

Smelling the air and detecting the approach of a thunderstorm, Diana replied, "Yes, it smells like rain."

Danae closed her eyes and again asked, "Do you smell that?"

Once again, her mother replied, "Yes, I think we're about to get wet. It smells like rain."

Still caught in the moment, Danae shook her head, patted her thin shoulders with her small hands and loudly announced, "No, it smells like Him. It smells like God when you lay your head on his chest."

Tears blurred Diana's eyes as Danae then happily hopped down to play with the other children before the rains came. Her daughter's words confirmed what Diana and all the members of the extended Blessing family had known, at least in their hearts, all along.

During those long days and nights of her first two months of her life when her nerves were too sensitive for them to touch her, God was holding Danae on his chest — and it is His loving scent that she remembers so well.

Nancy Miller
Columbia Homecare Group
Dallas, Texas

A SAINT MARCHES IN

Every April high atop the Cumberland Plateau of eastern Tennessee, dandelions and bluebells splash the countryside with a colorful welcome for each new spring, turning the plateau into a magnetic place of beauty, one difficult to leave behind.

Yet in early April 1996, Charles Buesing, 72, knew it was almost time for him to go.

Four months before, doctors had discovered a deadly lung cancer and predicted he had no more than six months to live. A practical man with a strong character, Mr. Buesing had accepted his fate, managing to keep both his spirits and strength strong as his last season of spring wildflowers bloomed around the house he shared with his second wife, Lizzie, in the tiny community of Byrdstown.

"I'll never forget the first time I saw him," says Tiffany Olive, 33, a counselor and bereavement coordinator at Columbia Hospice in nearby Livingston, who first met Mr. Buesing on Thursday, April 25.

"He was in the sunroom of his home, looking out the window, watching the birds playing out back. He looked real good and when we started talking, I could tell he was adjusted to his disease and his prognosis."

As she always does, Tiffany went down a long

checklist to see what the hospice might be able to do to help Mr. Buesing. To both her admiration and surprise, there didn't seem to be a single thing to do to help him. He had accepted his upcoming death with dignity, having already talked everything out with his family and friends, as well as plan his funeral.

"Not being able to do anything had never happened to me before," says Tiffany, whose lifelong dream — even before age 12 when she lost her own mother to cancer — was to become a social worker of some kind in order to help other people.

"I mean I was trying to help, but I wasn't getting anywhere because I couldn't find anything he needed from any of our services. So finally, I said, 'Well, if there was just one thing I could do for you, what would it be?'

"He looked at me, leaned forward and said, 'Get my daughter here before I die.' I said, 'Sure, no problem. Where is she?' "

Mr. Buesing paused a moment before responding, "California."

"Okay," Tiffany confidently said aloud, while her thoughts did a backward somersault. California? How in the world can I get his daughter all the way from California to Tennessee? But Tiffany didn't give away her thoughts, instead adding, "I'll do it."

Though Mr. Buesing was emotionally very close to both of his children, his son lived nearby but his daughter, Jeannine, lived more than 2,000 miles away in Santa Cruz. While they talked frequently by phone, they had been unable as of yet to come up with enough extra money for Jeannine to make the expensive trip to Tennessee, though she promised her father she would make it, "some way." Like the Buesings, Tiffany was not wealthy — at least not in a monetary way — but she had confidence that Mr. Buesing's health would hold steady for a few weeks until she figured out a plan for the trip.

Four days later on Monday, April 29, Tiffany walked into her office to the chilling news that Mr. Buesing's health had taken a drastic downward turn over the weekend. He was still at home, but he had only hours or days — not weeks to live.

"I panicked," Tiffany says squarely.

With a telephone and tenacity as her only tools of attack, she frantically began dialing the 800 numbers for several major airlines whose routes could immediately fly Jeannine from her Pacific Coast home to the Nashville International Airport, a two-hour car drive away from the Cumberland Plateau.

Tiffany's first round of calls brought dismal results. A regular round-trip ticket price was a small fortune, ranging from $1,380 to $1,400. But while talking to all the ticket agents, Tiffany realized the biggest barrier to better rates was the lack of a 14-day or more advance reservation. Calling each of the airlines back, she explained the ticket was for a medical emergency and, in turn, each of the carriers quoted prices in the $550 range.

"In a small town like ours where it's sometimes tough for some of us to find enough money to buy antibiotics, that was still way too much money for me to try to find," Tiffany recalls, in her ever-optimistic, yet matter-of-fact manner.

Desperate, she decided to call the airlines one more time. Instead of trying to grasp all the different fares of advance ticketing and special rates, she made up her mind to explain exactly what the situation was and hope for the best.

"I'm in a real bind here," Tiffany began, talking to a stranger by the name of Mr. Thompson on the 800 line, rushing to explain everything.

"As luck would have it, this Mr. Thompson told me his wife happened to be a nurse at a hospice, so he understood my problem. Of course that sparked his interest in helping me, and I thought at the time how lucky I was to have gotten through to him, out of all the people who answer the 800 numbers at all the different airlines."

After a few minutes on hold, Mr. Thompson returned, explaining that his supervisor had agreed to waive the 14-day advance and offer a discounted ticket price of $245.

"I'll take it!" Tiffany eagerly replied. But when he asked for her credit card number to make the purchase, she remembered her credit card was "maxed out." Explaining that she would have to call him back, Mr. Thompson gave her a special number in order to call him, personally, through the huge telephone bank of ticket agents.

After dialing her credit card company, Tiffany repeated her story, pleading with them to raise her credit limit high enough so that she could charge the ticket. And — in a world that is often perceived as coldly computerized — she was gratefully amazed when the charge card company agreed.

Without a minute to lose, Tiffany called Jeannine Buesing who rushed to the San Jose airport near her home and buckled her seat belt at noon Pacific time, a mere handful of hours after Tiffany began her frantic calls.

"I arrived in Nashville at nine o'clock that Monday night," Jeannine says. "My step-sister picked me up, and we drove straight to the house. It was 11 o'clock when we walked in. My father was laying on the bed. I said, 'I love you. I told you I would make it.' He sat up and said, 'I love you, too, baby.' Then he laid back down."

Within hours, Mr. Buesing's condition worsened further. With her stepmother and other family members, Jeannine rode in the car to take her father to Columbia Livingston Regional Hospital for the last time.

"I was in the back seat and he was in the front," Jeannine says. "He kept patting the back of the seat with his hand, and when I asked him what was wrong, he said, 'Baby, I can't touch you.' I reached up and held his hand until we got to the hospital."

A few hours later, Mr. Buesing lay in his hospital bed in a sedated haze. With the rest of his family close by, his wife was on one side of the bed holding his hand and Jeannine was on the other. As the two women talked to him of good times long past, Jeannine could see faint smiles cross her father's face. Then, when his breathing grew painfully difficult, they told him how much they loved him and urged him to "quit fighting and go ahead and go."

"When he stopped breathing, there was such a peaceful look on his face," Jeannine recalls. "Then the most incredible thing happened. All of a sudden my stepmother and I got this warmest feeling, like somebody had taken a warm blanket and wrapped it around us. We started crying and smiling at the same time because we felt so warm and peaceful, too."

Today, Tiffany shuns any and all words of praise for arranging the trip, saying she has always had "a lucky streak" and that luck led her to the man named Mr. Thompson — whose first name she never learned — and an understanding credit card company representative.

But back in California, Jeannine — who had to fly back home shortly after the funeral without ever having the opportunity to meet Tiffany in person —

"Tiffany Olive is a saint," Jeannine proclaims, flat-out, without a hint of a doubt. "I can't imagine how I would have felt then, or how I would feel now, if I hadn't been able to make the trip and hold my father's hand when he died.

"Because of Tiffany, I got that chance. I will never be able to thank her enough, though I will remember her, always and always. And whenever I think of her, which is often, I get the same feeling I felt at my father's bedside. I feel warm and peaceful just knowing there are people like Tiffany in this world."

Denise Elder
Columbia Homecare Livingston
Livingston, Tennessee

NO JOURNEY TOO LONG

For years, the giant silos towered harmlessly above the cold terrain of the Russian Ukraine, churning out energy for hundreds of miles beyond their solemn perch.

Then came April 26, 1986.

An explosion ripped the protective cover off one of the four nuclear reactors, gushing a foggy mountain of radioactive steam into the air. At least 31 people were killed and more than 100,000 others were evacuated as the vast fog swept across northern Europe. One of the worst fears of the 20th Century had become a reality — a catastrophic nuclear accident which would go down in the history books as simply "Chernobyl."

Eight years later and half a world away, Natalya Karpova — one of those evacuated from her home in Belarus, a republic of the former Soviet Union — thought she had escaped the frightening reach of the deadly fog. After immigrating to the United States in the early 1990s, she and her husband and their two young children were working hard to build a new life in the suburbs of Chicago.

But as the days of summer cooled into the fall of

1994, Natalya, a nurse with boundless energy, grew increasingly tired. At first, she cast it off to the rigors of working two jobs and tending to her family, but soon, she knew that whatever invisible sponge was soaking up all her strength went well beyond simple fatigue.

Still, the diagnosis was staggering.

Natalya — whose former home was a mere 60 kilometers away from Chernobyl — had "myelodysplasia," commonly known as pre-leukemia, an often swift-moving cancer which destroys bone marrow. While chemotherapy may prolong survival for several months, a bone marrow transplant using a highly matched donor is the only known cure for the killer disease.

The first doctor Natalya saw offered her little hope, treating her with weekly blood transfusions. And with no insurance, she knew of no other place to turn as she grew weaker and weaker. Then, by chance, a fellow nurse from the former Soviet Union whose own son had also fallen victim to Chernobyl but had been cured, recommended that Natalya make an appointment with Dr. Rose Catchatourian, director of the Bone Marrow Transplant Program at Columbia Michael Reese Hospital.

"I had never met a doctor like her," Natalya recalls. "From the very first appointment, she did everything to make me feel better and everything to help me."

As a pioneer in bone marrow transplants, Dr. Catchatourian instantly recognized both the severity and immediacy of Natalya's condition — and knowing the difficulties of finding perfect-match donors — the doctor was thrilled to learn that Natalya had a non-identical twin sister named Svetlana.

The only problem was that she still lived on the other side of the world.

Dr. Catchatourian — whose patients and co-workers say has a dauntless disregard for "practical" problems when it comes to helping others — dug in to help Natalya. Using phones, faxes and a dose of her compelling charm, the doctor sent the necessary information about Natalya to Svetlana's doctors in Belarus. The results they returned were perfect. Svetlana was healthy and her marrow was a 100 percent match. That left one last hurdle — getting Natalya's twin to the U.S. And again, Dr. Catchatourian stepped in. Within hours, she was on the telephone with the American Embassy in Minsk, and within weeks, Svetlana stepped off the plane in Chicago, her "compassionate" visa in hand.

The bone marrow transplant — which required a longthy, lonely hospital stay in isolation with chemotherapy and other treatments for Natalya but only a minor hospital visit for Svetlana — took place on March 24, 1995.

It was a complete success.

Now, looking back at her days near death, Natalya is still in awe of two women, her doctor and her sister.

"Dr. Catchatourian," Natalya says, haltingly, "I have no words for her because she did so much for me, she did everything for me. She never had any question not to help. She didn't care about anything, not the expenses, not the distance, nothing but to help me. Without her and my sister, I would not be here."

Because Svetlana had to leave her own young son behind to travel to America, she returned to Belarus shortly after the transplant. Before saying good-bye, Svetlana summed up what Natalya will forever be thankful for, a motto of sorts obviously shared by both Dr. Catchatourian and Natalya's twin sister.

"No journey is too long or too hard," Svetlana said, "to save someone else's life."

Geraldine Conrad
Columbia Michael Reese Hospital and Medical Center
Chicago, Illinois

MOO, TOO

Sheryl Belnap was sitting cross-legged on the floor tending to the wounded leg of Oval "Granny" Evans, one of her home health care patients, that soggy Texas day in January 1995.

"I couldn't see outside, but I could tell something was upsetting Granny," says Sheryl, a Columbia Homecare Lifeway nurse from Bastrop, Texas. "She asked me if I heard something, and that's when I noticed that the cows her grandson kept on the farm were making a strange noise.

"Granny said, 'I'm afraid there must be a snake in the barn.' "

Being a "city girl" from nearby Austin, Sheryl, 44, didn't know anything about cows or snakes or the possible results of having the two types of creatures together in a barn. Nor did she know quite how to handle Granny's request.

"There wasn't anyone else around but the two of us, so she asked me if I would take her pistol and go check for a snake," Sheryl recalls, the memory still close enough to stir a nervous laugh. "I didn't know what to say. Granny could barely move around, but I had never touched a gun before in my whole life.

"Finally, she told me where the gun was and I got the courage to pick it up. I was so flustered, I remember holding it out in front of me as far as I could and asking if there was a bullet in it."

There was, and the next thing Sheryl remembers is tromping out into the rain across the muddy field toward the barn with the pistol in one hand and an umbrella in the other.

"It was a good hike to the barn," she says. "When I got close to the cows, the ground was all nasty and my tennis shoes were soaked. Then I saw a bull, I mean a real big bull, with horns, eye-balling me. A big cow was lying on the ground close by, moaning real loud. I looked down at her and knew the problem wasn't a snake. She was trying to have a calf but it wasn't going real easy."

Putting the pistol aside — yet keeping her umbrella as her "weapon" to ward off the bull — Sheryl's natural, if rather unconventional "cow-side" manner, took over.

"I got down on the ground, started rubbing her belly and talking to her, trying to calm her down," Sheryl says. "She looked up at me with her big, beautiful cow eyes, and I could tell she knew I wanted to help her.

"Pretty soon, I knew if I was going to really help her have her baby, I'd have to get on the other side of her, which meant turning my back on the bull. I guess I thought about it a minute and figured there wasn't anything else to do, so I looked at him and got this feeling, I don't know from where, that he knew I was trying to help bring his new baby into the world. Then I just forgot about the bull."

Over the next long hour, Sheryl diagnosed, remedied and successfully helped the cow deliver a breech-birth calf, singing lullabies all the while.

Then Granny's grandson came barreling across the field in his red pickup and stopped beside Sheryl, who by that time was a "complete, awful mess."

"What are you doing?" he yelled. "Don't you know that bull could've killed you! They don't like people to start with, and they sure don't like them in times like this! You must be crazy, lady!"

Hours later back in the office writing her reports, Sheryl agreed with that appraisal of her state of mind. And since her barnyard services weren't something that could be billed, she fancifully filled out a form to record her "unscheduled" visit to the barnyard.

Offering the patient's name as "Cocoa" — the dark brown baby bull Granny insisted that Sheryl name — she went on to fill out the rest of the form. Under general comments, she wrote "mother in distress." Of the baby's skin description, she wrote "warm, sticky, yucky." Beside the type of sterile technique, she wrote, "To help cow bear large calf, no particular technique at all." To the assessment question, she wrote "calf understands mother's moo after several minutes of disorientation." And in the blank for future plans and goals, Sheryl wrote, "Let's Not Do This Again!"

Oval Evans passed away in the summer of 1996. Sheryl still misses her, but the memory of Granny that January day will always bring Sheryl a smile. And she still believes her safety that afternoon came from the unspoken trust the bull had that she was trying to help.

"Sometimes," Sheryl says, still laughing at herself, "we as human beings are a lot better off not knowing things that make us step back, rationalize and worry about things, like what that bull could have done to me.

"Sometimes, the best things happen when we just do things we feel we ought to do. And that's all I did, just tried to help."

Sherry Sanders
Columbia Homecare Lifeway
Bastrop, Texas

SAY GOOD MORNING, GRACE E.

In the small examination room, it sounded like a sonic boom.

"It was my chin hitting the floor when we found out we were going to have twins," laughs Dan Malinee. "I was sure the whole world heard it."

Like most new parents-to-be, Dan and his wife, Sally, were already thrilled that they were going to have a baby. And because Dan operates his own company from their home on the Missouri side of Kansas City, he felt fortunate to be able to be with his wife during all of her prenatal checkups, including the first ultra-sound exam three months into her pregnancy in late summer 1995.

"Having never been through anything like it before, we just went in and the technician was taking the sonogram and asking us questions," Dan explains.

"At one point she asked us if there was a history of twins in our families. We just figured it was another routine question they asked everyone.

"I said, 'No, not mine, what about you, Sal?' Sally said no, too. Then the lady looked at us and said, 'Well, there is now.' That's when my chin hit the floor. I said, 'Oh my Lord, Sally, we've got our own George and Gracie.' It was wonderful."

At that early date — with no way yet to determine the sex of either twin — Dan's spur-of-the-moment comment was no more than his elation over the exciting news.

But the nicknames stuck, thanks to the Malinees' fondness for the superstar comedic couple, George Burns and his late wife, Gracie Allen.

Dan and Sally, though only in their 30s, had long appreciated the humor of George and Gracie, from recordings of the old radio days to shows from the early days of television.

"George was just super, Gracie was a real genius and together they were fabulous," Dan says.

"We loved them, so from that very first day when we were told we were going to have twins, Sally and I referred to the babies with those nicknames, at least between ourselves."

The Malinees were halfway through the pregnancy before the sexes of the twins were revealed — a boy and a girl — and that's when Dan and Sally first seriously thought of naming the twins after the dynamic Burns and Allen entertainment duo.

And then, without telling anyone the sexes of the twins or their intended names, the couple soon settled on "George Spencer" — from Sally's mother's maiden name of Spencer for their new son — and "Grace Elizabeth," to put an "E" after Grace for their new daughter.

As life would have it, George Burns, at age 100, passed on to be with his beloved wife in early March 1996.

Three days later on March 12, 1996 — the same day and hour that Burns was laid to rest — doctors at Columbia Overland Park Regional Medical Center delivered George Malinee into the world at 11:54 a.m., followed exactly one minute later by his sister Grace E. Malinee.

Both twins were exceptionally healthy.

And Dan and Sally, in keeping with their own bond of love and humor, added a special twist to announce the birth of their twins.

Printed to represent theatrical tickets — complete with perforated "seating" stubs with individual numbers — the birth announcement was unique.

It read:

Dan and Sally Malinee
proudly present,
in conjunction with
Overland Park Regional Medical Center,
A Sally Malinee Production of
"GEORGE & GRACE E."
LIVE

George Spencer   Grace Elizabeth
5 lbs/ 2 oz/ 18"   2 lbs/ 9 oz/ 14"
A two-act crying, cooing,
comedy performance on stage
PREMIER SHOWING: MARCH 12, 1996
Straight from a nine-month engagement
in the "Boom-Boom Womb"
of the fabulous "Hotel Sal"
Produced by Sally Malinee,
Directed by Dr. Randy Sheridan,
Designed by Dan Malinee

Along with a full collection of Burns and Allen memorabilia, the Malinees made sure to keep the ticket stubs marked "#1" and "#2" for their own new superstars.

Fran Ford Jacques
Columbia Overland Park Regional Medical Center
Overland Park, Kansas

ANGEL, UNAWARE

Brenda Gail Glover did more than live life — she hugged every second of it, tight.

As a young woman, she loved the laughter of little children. She adored unicorns. She would not abide with anything that made her mother cry. She was star-struck by the country music group, Alabama. And right before her 26 fleeting years of life came to an end, she promised to save her friends seats in Heaven.

"Brenda could find beauty and happiness in the smallest things," says Beverly Keller, a Columbia Homecare Coosa Valley nurse-turned-best-friend who spent countless hours with Brenda through the spring, summer and fall of 1995, up until the day Brenda died of ovarian cancer that November.

"She taught me more in the time I knew her than I have learned in all my other years put together. Brenda didn't think of it this way, but to me, she was a real angel, unaware of the impact she had on those of us who were fortunate enough to have the chance to know her."

Back in early 1995, Brenda was living with her mother, Lou Ella Glover, in their modest home in Fairmount in northeastern Georgia. The mother and daughter also worked together in a production unit of the textile manufacturing company of Springs Industries in the nearby town of Calhoun.

Sadly, by the time Brenda's condition was finally diagnosed, the cancer had already invaded her body to the point that there was no hope of a cure.

Trying to hold on — as much or more for her mother than herself — Brenda underwent all the medical treatments her doctors prescribed. And even as her long, sandy blonde hair gave way to baldness and baseball caps, not even the strong doses of chemotherapy could take away the sparkle in her eyes.

"Not once, not one single time, did Brenda ever complain about the physical and emotional pain she was going through," Beverly remembers. "The only thing she worried about was her mother.

"She would say, 'Do whatever you have to do to me, but just don't make Mama cry.' She was simply incredible."

When word of Brenda's condition swept through the small communities near her home and the executive suites of Spring Industries, a virtual flood of love flowed her way. Area churches chipped in so that Brenda could have cable TV, an air-conditioner and pre-paid utility bills. Employees of the home health group pitched in to purchase a new set of sheets and a soft comforter to create what Brenda called "the most beautiful bed I've ever seen." Hundreds of her former co-workers at Spring Industries, many of whom she had never met, donated countless dollars to pay for her costly medical treatments. And the corporate side of Spring Industries paid the way for Brenda to be taken by special van to a company-sponsored concert in South Carolina, coincidentally headlined by Brenda's favorite group, Alabama.

In mid-concert, the musicians asked Brenda to come on stage. Weak but unwilling to miss that extraordinary second of her life, Brenda — amidst the wild applause and tears of the audience of 14,000 workers who knew what she was fighting — smiled with such brilliance that the spotlights seemed to dim as each musical member of Alabama gave her a kiss on the cheek.

Her worldly dream had come true.

Then as the first days of November rolled around, it became clear that no amount of medicine or anything else could keep Brenda in this life. So to save her mother from having to deal with the final arrangements alone, Brenda made a few decisions, herself. She would be buried in her high school prom dress, a long, light green satin grown with white lace trim. If possible, she would like a picture of a unicorn to take along with her. Beyond that, Brenda had no other wishes except trying to make sure her departure would be as painless as possible for her mother.

Beverly and other friends immediately set out to make Brenda's final farewell wishes come true. After talking to Brenda's mother, Beverly was explaining to her friend, neighbor and funeral home director, Eddie Brannon, the simple service Brenda wanted.

"When I mentioned the picture of a unicorn, Eddie suddenly stopped me," Beverly recalls. "He seemed real surprised and asked, 'What?' I told him again how Brenda loved unicorns, and Eddie said, 'This is too much. A couple of weeks ago, a man walked into the funeral home, handed me a picture and told me to hold onto it because a young girl would soon be coming to the funeral home and would be needing it.'

"Eddie said it was a picture of a young woman in a flowing gown with a lantern in her hand and a unicorn behind her," Beverly says, swallowing hard. "For no real reason, he had it framed then set it aside, not knowing what to do with it. Then, when I told him about Brenda, it was just too much. Too overwhelming. Too amazing."

A few nights later, Beverly was one of the people called to accompany Brenda to the hospital for the last time. When they reached the emergency room, Brenda leaned over close and told her, "If I don't ever see you again here, I'll save you a seat in Heaven."

Once in her hospital room, a doctor walked in and said, "Brenda, I wish I could give you a miracle, but I don't have one."

True to her form of finding the best of everything in this life, Brenda said, "Okay, but you all are gonna take care of my Mama, aren't you?"

After everyone assured her that they would, Brenda died a few days later.

At her funeral, the picture of the angel with a unicorn was placed inside her casket. And Jim Cole, a pastor and human resources director for Spring Industries, offered the eulogy. After describing Brenda and mentioning her love of children and unicorns, he ended with words to help soothe her mother's tears, words Brenda certainly would have approved.

"So, some quiet night when you are missing Brenda, as you will just like the rest of us, listen close. You might just hear, echoing from some corner of Heaven, the laughter of children playing and Brenda saying, 'Look, look, children! It's a unicorn!' "

Renee Webb

Columbia Homecare Coosa Valley

Rome, Georgia

ACCIDENTAL BLESSING

The blast of the .44 magnum thundered through the Snake River Valley in eastern Idaho that Wednesday in May 1996. The bullet, a 250-grain hollow point, struck Ann Clark, 10, slamming in through her right chest and out of her lower back.

For a split-second, her brother, John, 12, stared in disbelief at the gun in his hand. Home alone, the two youngsters had been playing with the handgun, believing it was unloaded.

Now, the horrendous hole in Ann's chest and stream of blood proved them terribly wrong.

John scrambled upstairs and dialed 911. Beyond the bullet, he knew that time and distance were other enemies his sister was fighting in their home in the beautiful yet remote region near Rexburg, within view of Wyoming's Grand Tetons. It was a good five miles to the small hospital in town, and another 30 miles to a larger hospital in Idaho Falls.

Soon, John heard the siren screaming down the lonely road, and then watched the paramedics swarm around Ann.

Minutes later, Steve and Ruth Ann Clark — parents of nine children, with Ann and John the youngest — rushed in. As a devoutly religious family,

Steve wanted to take a few moments to offer a special blessing for Ann as she was placed on the stretcher, but the paramedics said there was no time.

Steve said a silent prayer as they all sped out the door.

"I told my wife we had to get John," Steve says. "At first, she thought I was upset with him or something, but I told her goodness no, that John needed our love then as much as Ann did."

Guns had always been a natural part of the Clarks' life, with Steve and his sons hunting deer and elk for food. Normally, all the guns were kept empty and locked in a storage room, but the loaded handgun had been inadvertently left out.

"I knew John needed to know that accidents happen," Steve says. "As painful as it was for him and for all of us, I wanted to keep him from getting caught up in guilt."

At the local hospital, a team of more than a dozen emergency room specialists quickly made the decision that Ann's best chances were to stabilize then airlift her to Columbia Eastern Idaho Regional Medical Center, 30 miles away, where emergency room physician Dr. Robert Wagner and cardiovascular surgeon Dr. Fred Stockinger would be waiting.

So at 6:59 p.m., an Air Idaho Rescue helicopter,

with Ann aboard, touched down in Idaho Falls. Within 20 minutes, she was whisked into surgery.

"Almost four hours later, Dr. Stockinger came out of the operating room," Steve recalls. "He said, 'The bad news is that your daughter was shot. The good news is that everything after that went as well as it possibly could have, from getting help in time and then getting her here. If I could have plotted a route for the bullet to do as least damage as possible, I couldn't have done better than the bullet.' "

At that moment, Steve says he knew that "the Lord had stepped in" and saved Ann's life.

"I had never been so grateful in my life," he says.

For Ann and her many family members who gathered from other states to be close by her side, the hours following surgery were difficult. The most immediate concern was fluid building in her lungs, threatening potentially fatal pneumonia.

But her family — after hearing that extremely few people, anywhere, under any situations survive a point-blank .44 magnum bullet — encouraged the young girl, saying, "If you can beat that bullet, you sure can beat pneumonia."

She responded by following her doctor's order to cough to expel the fluid — an extremely painful procedure, since the bullet had cracked several ribs.

"Ann is a strong, courageous girl," her father says. "She would cough, then cry, cough, then cry, over and over again, until the threat of pneumonia was gone."

A few days after the accident, Ann's family was gathered around her hospital room, offering both silent and spoken prayers and praise that her young life had been spared.

"I looked around Ann's room and got this wonderful feeling," Steve says. "I realized that if she hadn't have made it, that moment would have been about the time we all would have been gathered around her for her viewing, saying things about what a great little girl she had been and how much we all would miss her.

"It was like feeling a little bit of Heaven, a real warmth of still having her there with us, knowing how close we'd come to losing her. The Lord stepped in for her and for the rest of us. Her recovery was such an enormous blessing for John, too. It would have been so hard for him if Ann had died. The Lord was so incredibly kind."

Surprising her doctors, Ann was well enough to return home within a week of the accident. And though the Clark family still has guns in their home, the weapons — checked to make sure they are unloaded — and the ammunition are now locked away in separate places so that the events of that horrible day are never replayed in their house, again.

But beyond those practical matters, Steve has seen changes in his youngest son and daughter that he attributes to the horror they went though.

"John is maturing in a way I never noticed before," Steve says. "He's still happy and a lot of fun, but he has a new awareness that there are serious things and serious feelings out there in life. And Ann has developed a new sweetness, an empathy and caring for people that wasn't there before.

"The terrible accident has turned into a blessing, beyond comprehension, for all of us."

Ronald Butler

Columbia Eastern Idaho Regional Medical Center
Idaho Falls, Idaho

FRIED FISH FOR CHARLOTTE

After 15 years as a nurse at Jacksonville's busy Columbia Orange Park Medical Center in north Florida, Dianne Johnson thought she had "seen it all."

Then came Charlotte.

It was a rushed morning in 1996 when medical attendants wheeled a stretcher into the hospital.

It appeared to be so light, it could easily have been carrying no weight beyond the rumpled white sheets. But as it drew closer, Dianne saw a wispy braid of long, white hair and then the form of a very elderly, feeble woman.

Taking the chart from the attendants, Dianne glanced down at the woman's name, Charlotte, and her age — 105.

"Did any family member come with her?" Dianne asked one of the attendants, who had transported the woman there from a nursing home.

"No," he replied shortly, walking away down the long hospital hallway.

Turning to her patient, Dianne said gently, "I'm going to be the nurse who gets you ready for surgery."

A faint moan was Charlotte's only reply.

"Do you know where you are?" Dianne asked.

Another moan.

"Do you understand why you are here?" she went on softly.

Very slowly, Charlotte turned her thin face toward Dianne, and in an irate screech, yelled:

"I'm an old lady! I'm cold. Cover me up!"

Racing for blankets, Dianne obeyed, wrapping them around Charlotte's thin form and placing a pillow at her back. Though pale and splotched with the brown marks of more than ten decades of life, the old woman's skin was silken to the touch. But as Dianne adjusted the blankets, she spotted the virulent black mark on Charlotte's right toe. Gangrene — the root of her extreme pain — and the urgent need for surgery.

If Charlotte was to live, she would have to do it without her right leg.

At that moment in her own mind, Dianne thought about the great advances in medical technology of the 20th Century which allow life to be significantly prolonged. But she also wondered if 105 was too old for anyone to have to withstand such major surgery as the amputation of a limb.

Charlotte already had lived well beyond the normal life expectancy, and Dianne fleetingly wondered, who, if anyone, should decide when life has ended its own natural progression.

As a professional, Dianne quickly put her personal musings aside as she proceeded to prepare Charlotte for the surgical removal of her right leg, above the knee. With each move she made, Dianne tried her best to explain everything to Charlotte. But between her new surroundings and acute pain, it was clear that Charlotte could not sign the necessary permission forms for the doctor and hospital to conduct the surgery.

On her chart, a cousin was listed as Charlotte's next of kin.

Rushing around, the staff found a phone number for the cousin. The line was busy. And the minutes ticked away.

Amidst their efforts, Charlotte suddenly grabbed Dianne and pulled her close.

"I'm an old lady!" she bellowed into the nurse's ear. "Do you know how old I am?"

Time, precious time, whirred by as Dianne assured her that she did, trying to keep Charlotte as comfortable as possible.

At last, permission was obtained. Charlotte was rushed into the operating room. Dianne watched her go.

After an entire morning with Charlotte, the medical center seemed strangely silent without her nearby. And as Dianne went about her job tending to other patients, thoughts of Charlotte swirled around in her head like a song she couldn't quite get out of her mind.

An avid genealogist of her own African-American family, Dianne knew she would love to listen to the tales Charlotte most certainly could spin about the life she had led over the past century-plus-five-years.

Was she the child of a slave? Did she work in the fields as a girl, share-cropping with her family? What had she seen on her walks down dusty roads to church and back? Had she gone to a one-room schoolhouse to learn how to read, or was an education of any kind even an option for young Charlotte so long ago?

Dianne thought of her own grandmother, comparing her life to the one Charlotte had led. She wondered if Charlotte had ever gotten a kick out of Duke Ellington's music, or swayed her young hips to Bessie Smith's loud and rowdy blues tunes. And of course Charlotte was still young — just in her seventies — when Rosa Parks refused a seat at the back of a bus, giving Dr. Martin Luther King Jr. his peaceful ammunition to ignite sit-ins and marches to demand the most basic civil rights Charlotte had been denied all her life. Had she marched, herself, or watched Dr. King on television? Had she beamed with ancient pride in having lived long enough to see those once unimagined dreams of equality coming true?

There was so much Dianne wanted to ask Charlotte.

Swamped with those thoughts, Dianne found herself looking at her watch much more frequently than usual that day. Charlotte had already been in surgery at least an hour as midday passed. The early afternoon seemed to inch by so slowly that Dianne was amazed at herself for being so touched by a woman she had known less than a day — a fact that dispelled, forever, her notion that as a nurse, she'd "seen it all."

Finally, hours later, the time arrived for Dianne to check on Charlotte in the recovery room.

While the surgery had gone well, Dianne didn't know what to expect as she made her way into the dimly-lit room. Suddenly, across the way, a thin hand waved at her.

Charlotte — waving and smiling!

With medication to ease the pain, Charlotte was the real Charlotte, making direct eye contact and ready to tackle the world, yet again.

"Do they fry fish in here?" Charlotte yelled to Dianne. "I'm 105 years old, and I ought to be able to get fish if I want to!"

Dianne smiled almost as wide as Charlotte.

Months later, Charlotte was back in her nursing home, almost as spry as ever, while awaiting her next birthday.

"That first day when I first saw Charlotte," Dianne says, "I wondered if we were interrupting life's natural progression. And I wondered if her body could withstand the trauma of anesthesia and surgery.

"But as I look at her now, I see that Charlotte has a strong will and a taste for life. And I know she's going to be just fine."

One other thing Charlotte is doing again these days is feeding herself.

Fish, no doubt. Fried crispy on the outside, with tender flakes inside, just as it should be.

After all, as Charlotte never hesitates to tell anyone, when a lady is 105 years old, she ought to be able to get what she wants.

And Dianne — who learned so much about herself and life through Charlotte — couldn't agree more.

Margaret Wright
Columbia North Florida Division
Jacksonville, Florida

TRAGIC TO MAGIC

One day when Hannah Alyse Cervantes is old enough, she will learn about the exceptional circumstances which occurred during the first month of her life. And her aunt and uncle, now her new parents, only hope they can convey the outpouring of love that rallied round them and Hannah in the hours and days after the tragedy on May 2, 1996 in southern Texas.

At the time, Linda and Carlos Cervantes — along with Linda's younger sister, Elaine Earnest, who was single — all worked at Methodist Hospital in San Antonio, where Carlos was director of pulmonary services and the sisters were nurses.

Linda and Carlos already had two grown children, Aaron, 26, and Brandon, 16. But Elaine, 39, had given birth only 12 days earlier to a new daughter, Hannah. Like their close family, the tight-knit staff at the hospital had been thrilled by the new addition to their lives.

Then, Elaine died instantly in a one-car traffic accident.

For a heartbeat, everyone who knew and loved her didn't know what to say, then a question broke the silence.

"Who will take care of Hannah?"

Under the family's circumstances, it was clear the infant's aunt and uncle would be her new parents.

"Linda and I didn't have to talk about it at all," Carlos says. "We just knew we would take care of Hannah, not out of obligation or responsibility, but because that's what we wanted to do."

The adoption papers were filed. Hannah moved in with the Cervantes on May 12 — Mother's Day 1996. And from the beginning, it was clear that Hannah's extended family would include the entire staff at Methodist Hospital.

"Their support was unbelievable," Linda says. "They gave us emotional support, monetary support and support in many other ways. They even had a beautiful memorial service for Elaine at the hospital. I appreciate very much the respect they showed for my sister and how much they cared for her."

Carlos agrees, saying, "The way everyone reached out to us has strengthened my belief in mankind. Working in health care, you see death often, but sometimes you don't realize how close we all are to death. In the blink of an eye, you can be gone."

Nowadays, Hannah has adjusted well to her new home and parents. Carlos works days, then when Linda leaves the house for her 3 p.m. shift, her mother, Hazel, takes care of Hannah until Carlos gets home and, with the help of son Brandon, takes over for the night.

Still, Elaine has not — nor will she ever be — forgotten.

Her photograph has a prominent place in the Cervantes' home for everyone to see, especially Hannah.

"I don't know exactly when the time will come for me to tell Hannah that Elaine was her mommy and I am her mommy, too," Linda says. "I just want Hannah to know what kind of person her mother was and that we miss her very much."

In the meantime, the Cervantes have discovered that having a baby in their lives again has spurred an unexpected surprise.

It was only a few weeks before Elaine's death that Carlos had mentioned to Linda that he missed all the fun and excitement that comes with sharing special times alongside the wondrous wide eyes of young children.

"We loved those days when our sons were young," Carlos says, "that magic that comes with a child experiencing new things like the excitement over birthdays and Christmas.

"Now, because Hannah is in our life, we are so very fortunate because we're getting an opportunity to recapture that magic, to live those days of magic, once again."

Steve Finley
Columbia Methodist Healthcare System
San Antonio, Texas

THE CRUMLEY HOUSE

One particular red-brick, ranch-style home in the foothills of the Great Smoky Mountains is more than a house.

It's living proof of a mother's vow to transcend tragedy by creating a haven of hope for others.

June Ford Barrett's long journey began on what would otherwise have been a lovely September day in 1981 in Johnson City, Tennessee. That was when the youngest of her two daughters — Lori Beth Ford, 14, a lively, popular, straight-A student at Liberty Bell Junior High with auburn hair and blue eyes — made a simple decision most every teenager makes, or is at least tempted to do.

Only months away from getting her driver's permit, Lori decided to take a quick trip in the family car with two friends to collect money the young students had raised for a school trip, then return home before her mother and stepfather ever knew.

But driving along a winding two-lane highway, Lori lost control on a sharp curve. The car finally came to a rest, upside down, in a tangle of shattered glass and mangled steel.

While her two friends sustained frightening, yet minor injuries, the front left side of Lori's skull was crushed.

"Her brain damage is very, very severe," the doctor told June and her husband, Steve Barrett, as soon as they reached the emergency room. "We don't believe she will live through the night."

The doctor kept talking. June had heard enough.

Standing beside Lori's hospital bed next to all the machines that were keeping her daughter alive, June's mind was screaming though the news was too fresh for her mouth to form any words. Instead, a motion picture of memories of her beautiful, dynamic daughter sped through her mind — Lori as a baby, Lori learning to walk, Lori water skiing, Lori as a cheerleader, Lori riding horses, Lori dancing, Lori laughing, Lori just being Lori.

It was when those flashbacks ebbed that the reality sank in, deep.

"Lori was about to die," June recalls, "or if she lived, they said she would be a vegetable. That's when I asked for a miracle. I said, 'God, please, if you give me a miracle, I promise to use our lives as a witness to you to help other people.' That night, at that moment, that was all I knew to do."

Lori lived through the night, then the next few weeks, though she remained in a coma.

"It was about six weeks after the accident," June recalls, "when one of the doctors told me, 'Lori is not going to get any better. You need to start thinking in terms of putting her in a home because you need to get on with your life.'

"I guess that doctor and everybody else around there thought I was crazy, but I would not give up. Neither would the other members of our family or her friends. I stayed with her 18 hours a day, and her father, James Ford, would stay with her the other six while I went home to change.

"And we did everything. We had parties in her room. We hung posters on the walls. We played music she liked. We put flowers all over the place. And every weekday afternoon, the hospital corridor looked more like a school hallway when all her friends filed in to see her."

Right before Christmas, four months after the accident on Lori's 15th birthday, her family and friends threw an all-day party. By nightfall, as June and Steve leaned over each side of Lori's bed to say they were going to run out for a quick supper, Lori — in the first sign of activity of any kind — tried to sit up and move her legs to the side of the bed, trying to go with them.

"We finally knew then that she could hear us," June says, still unable to recall the moment without the smile of the proudest of parents.

The miracle June asked for was happening, but ever so slowly. After seven months at the hospital, Lori was released and taken to the nearest rehabilitation center, over four hours away in Virginia. But despite June's constant visits during which Lori seemed to make small slices of progress, Lori did nothing when June wasn't present.

After six weeks, June brought Lori home — hiring nurses to help with a homebound rehabilitation program. And inch-by-inch, the miracle marched on.

Twelve months after the accident, Lori relearned how to walk.

After fourteen months, her feeding tube was removed when she relearned how to eat real food. And after sixteen months, Lori relearned how to say her first words — "raisin" and "mama ... mama!"

Then the years crept by.

When her class graduated from high school, the school awarded Lori an honorary diploma. As her friends went off to colleges and careers, Lori attended special education classes at another school for four more years until she reached the maximum age to attend public schools.

That's when her mother realized they were facing yet another major hurdle — finding enough activities and social interaction for Lori to continue her slow climb into her "new" life.

"So we went looking for a nice, private, live-in rehabilitation center where we could visit her regularly but allow Lori to have a real life, too," June says.

After searching the state, they finally found one near Nashville where she knew Lori would continue to thrive in between her visits.

"I said, okay, this is a lovely place with a great program, so she'll like it here. How much is it a year?

"They said $300,000. I was knocked backwards. Three hundred thousand dollars a year? I mean, we'd already used up all the insurance money long ago, and they were asking for $300,000 a year! That's the moment I knew I had to do something. I didn't know what, but something, not just for Lori but for all the other young people like her."

June's plan to "do something" suddenly switched into fast-forward. In 1990, she formed a committee in Johnson City to look at ways to open and operate a five-day-a-week learning and training center for young adults with head injuries. While June began writing proposals for federal grants, she says "other little miracles" started popping up.

First, John Crysel, chief executive officer of the local Columbia North Side Hospital, called to say the hospital had just purchased 15 acres for expansion and the future of a red-brick, ranch-style house on the property was in question. The former owners of the property, Joe and Virginia Crumley, gladly offered their enthusiasm for June to use the house. And the county commission, after hearing of her project, deeded a corner of land for June's dream.

So, in July 1992, with countless other donations

from labor to materials, The Crumley House — named by June to give it a "warm, cozy feeling" — first opened its doors.

Lori, however, was not one of its first members because her mother knew there were other young adults who needed the service more immediately than her daughter. But a year later, Lori joined the group she now "loves."

While she has limitations if compared to her "old" life, Lori is now a beautiful young woman who strives to get the best out of everything.

And The Crumley House, which serves about 15 members at any given time and is currently in the planning stages of opening a larger facility complete with residential care for nominal fees, is highly respected as a model program to emulate across the United States.

"I've had lots and lots of help from lots and lots of friends," June says, in her ever-present, modest way.

"And you know, I got my miracle, so I had a promise to keep."

Barbara Deere
Columbia North Side Hospital
Johnson City, Tennessee

JOY OF SURPRISE

Everything was right on target in the summer of 1995.

A minister for 34 years, Dr. Gerald Freeman, 62, and his wife, Karen, 43, had decided 1996 would be the year Gerald would step down from his pastoral duties so that they could "retire" to become full-time missionaries in the central American country of Costa Rica.

Then came the first surprise in August 1995.

With two grown children in their 20s, Gerald and Karen were happily shocked to learn they were going to have a new baby.

"Oh my goodness," was all Gerald could muster aloud, as his thoughts swirled in thankful amazement at having a new baby bouncing into his life at such a late date.

By the early summer of 1996 — with excitement building toward Karen's September due date — she urged Gerald to go ahead, as planned, to lead a 10-day youth mission to Costa Rica. Walking out their front door in Montgomery, Alabama, on July 7, 1996, Gerald's last laughing words were, "Don't you have this baby until I get back."

Then came the second surprise eight days later.

With Gerald thousands of miles away, Karen's

blood pressure spiraled and other vital signs dipped dangerously low. Her doctors knew the only way to save her life — and hopefully, the life of her infant — was to perform an immediate cesarean. And so on July 15, 1996, the newest member of the Freeman family was born at Columbia East Montgomery Medical Center.

"When they called and told me they were both all right," Gerald says, "I was overjoyed, but I felt so helpless being so far away. I was just so thankful for the wonderful doctors and nurses at the hospital who literally saved my wife and our new baby. Without their skills, their commitment and their enthusiasm, I knew I probably would never have had a chance to see my new baby."

By long distance, Karen and Gerald agreed on their baby's name.

Then, with pen in hand, Gerald wrote these words to his new daughter.

A Letter To My Newborn Baby Far Away
2:30 a.m., July 17, 1996
Costa Rica

Dear Joy Lynne,
Well, I am thousands of miles away, and you

slipped right into our world without me. I am so sorry that I was not there to welcome you. I should have been by Mama's side, but I was about our Father's business helping children in another part of the world.

Welcome to the planet Earth, sweetheart! I look so forward to seeing you and holding you. We didn't plan on your arrival so early, but we are glad you are here. I feel your life will be such a blessing to us.

I am so excited about sharing life with you! I long to teach you about birds, dogs, butterflies, ducks and sharing the beauty of God's world with you.

You will be such a buddy for Mama and me as we travel the world for Jesus. We want you to see, to grow and to glow, as you experience all the wonders God has in store for you. We'll hug you and make you feel so welcome. We'll rock you, sing to you and, yes, we'll probably spoil you rotten.

Mama and I pray you will come to know the Jesus we know. To serve Him and love Him with all your heart. To experience His love and grace and beauty.

What a thrilling life it has been for Mama and me. Nevertheless, welcome to our world! It is a joy I have longed for, and that is why we named you Joy.

We look forward to the smiles, chuckles, giggles and laughter you will bring to our hearts.

I don't know how much longer I will walk God's green Earth. But sweetheart, I promise to give you the very best I have to offer. To make every day you live one of excitement, wonder and adventure.

God bless you, little Joy! Live your life with all the zest you can. Give God 100 percent of your best, and God will explode the wonders of this world before your eyes in such a way that you will live every day with a smile on your lips and a song in your heart.

Love,

Dad

While the surprises in the Freemans' life have temporarily postponed their dream of serving as missionaries to Costa Rica, their plan is still solidly in place.

Planning, anew, to make the move in 1997, their smiles give away their constant amazement that they will truly be traveling with Joy.

John Melton
Columbia East Montgomery Medical Center
Montgomery, Alabama

CYNDI'S LASTING WISH

If there ever came a time when Cyndi Hartman knew she would be unable to save her own life, she never let on. Nor did she ever give up.

If anything, the closer her body inched toward death, the harder she wished for ways to open the minds of others to one simple fact — how easy it is for someone to save someone else's life.

And now, her friends are determined to make sure Cyndi's last wish becomes a lasting one.

Up until December 1995, Cyndi — a strikingly attractive 38-year-old critical care nurse at Tucson's Columbia Northwest Medical Center in the dusty desert region of southern Arizona — lived a life packed with her patients, family and friends. She had only recently completed course work for her bachelor's degree in nursing and was deciding her next educational step when a nagging fatigue crept into her high-energy lifestyle, sending her to the doctor for a checkup.

Within days, a diagnosis was made. Cyndi was dying of a bone marrow disease.

Being a nurse, she knew her only chance at recovery would be a marrow transplant — she also knew her odds of finding a match were bleak, at best. Beyond a minuscule pool of donor volunteers nationally, even those numbers plummeted because of her genetic makeup of partial Hispanic descent.

And that's when Cyndi's crusade began.

"Beginning in January, Cyndi worked endlessly, through faltering health, to organize blood drives in search of donors," says Dorothy Sawyer, chief nursing officer at the medical center.

"But Cyndi's plea was not only in hopes of finding a donor for herself. She wanted to help others like herself by adding as many donors as possible to the national file."

One of the most important points Cyndi wanted the world to know is that marrow donations are relatively simple. They are usually less than hour-long procedures. They are usually done on an outpatient basis. And they leave the vast majority of donors with only a fleeting soreness, if any discomfort at all — very little effort in exchange for saving someone's life.

Thanks to Cyndi, her medical center conducted its largest donor drive, ever, in February 1996 — testing and typing 157 donors in one single day.

And thanks to Cyndi's continuing crusade, by July 1996, over 900 new volunteer donors from the area — including 500 from Hispanic descent — added their names to the National Marrow Donor

Registry.

Around the same time, Dorothy visited Cyndi's room during one of her increasingly frequent hospitalizations.

"Even though this very vivacious woman was pounds thinner and was struggling for breath," Dorothy remembers, "she refused to give up. She said, 'I have too much work to do.'

"But on July 24, 1996, Cyndi died. Even though her wish for a donor for herself never materialized, she kept fighting in hopes that others might live. And due to her efforts, others will live."

To make Cyndi's wish a lasting one, her co-workers and friends now do everything they can to keep Cyndi's quest flourishing — urging everyone to take a few minutes out of their busy lives to place their names on the marrow donor list.

"If Cyndi were still here to say this herself," Dorothy adds, "she would say this.

" 'People need to know how easy it can be to save somebody's life! We need you!' "

Dorothy Sawyer, RN, MN
Columbia Northwest Medical Center
Tucson, Arizona

MEDICINAL SNAILS

Ten hours of the most modern medical maneuvers came first.

Then came the age-old-creatures, bluntly defined in dictionaries as slimy "worms."

But together, on March 16, 1996, the two seemingly extremely distant, medicinal cousins came together to mend the wound of a 10-year-old boy named Isaac Fawcett.

The need for the divergent medical merger began that Saturday morning when Isaac and his brother Benjamin, 9, were helping their father spruce up the lawn around their home in Florida's Gulf Coast city of St. Petersburg. It was clear that the pruning effort was needed most at the overgrown Jacaranda tree in the backyard. So, as their father snipped away the large branches with sharp, long-handled shears, his sons held the branches for him to chop them into smaller bits.

Abruptly, Benjamin screamed, "Daddy! You cut his finger off! You cut Isaac's finger off!"

Looking down at his oldest son, David Fawcett saw the blood and knew it was true.

The shears had severed the thumb on Isaac's left hand, having sliced squarely through the knuckle. Drawing Isaac's hand up and pressing it against his own chest to try to stop the bleeding, David, the pastor of a St. Petersburg church, thought, "My God! What have I done?"

Then he said a prayer for his son as he hurried Isaac toward the car for the five-minute trip to the emergency room.

Hearing the frightened cries, a neighbor rushed over to help. Seeing what had happened, he placed Isaac's severed thumb into a glass filled with ice, to send along to the hospital.

Once there, as an IV was inserted to prepare Isaac for surgery, an imperative call was placed to Dr. Robert Rehnke, a renowned plastic surgeon who was spending that Saturday at home with his family. Whisking out his front door, the doctor was at the hospital 30 minutes later.

Then began the 10 long hours of painstaking surgery to reattach Isaac's severed thumb.

As the hours edged by, David and his wife, Marian, were given sporadic updates on their son's condition and the progress of the surgery.

"They kept telling us that because Isaac's thumb was so small, the doctor was having a hard time connecting the vein," Marian says. "They were able to connect the tendons and the artery, but the vein was difficult.

"Finally, after all the long hours, they were unable to reconnect the vein, so they sent Isaac to the recovery room."

Later, the surgeon sat down with the Fawcetts and their son to explain the next obstacle Isaac was facing. Without the vein reconnected, while blood could easily be pumped into his thumb, there was no medical gadget to make the blood flow out freely as it would normally circulate.

"Dr. Rehnke was so kind," Marian remembers. "He is such a wonderful, caring, dedicated man, and he told us that the most important thing was to keep the circulation going in Isaac's thumb. To do that, he started talking about using something called medicinal snails.

"Before he could finish, Isaac said, 'You're talking about leeches, aren't you?' I think the doctor was a little surprised when Isaac asked, but he smiled and told Isaac yes, that was exactly right."

The doctor went on to explain that these "snails," when simply laid on top of Isaac's wounded thumb, would naturally draw the blood out, completing the circulation cycle until his thumb healed enough to function on its own.

Isaac, who looked at the treatment as a sort of

adventure, eagerly agreed.

Because of the relative rarity of their use, the hospital had to order the batch of "medicinal snails" to be flown in from New York.

"Their" jet arrived at the airport about 12 hours later, and the true healing — and fun — began.

Over the next few days at regular intervals, a fresh, flat leech was placed on Isaac's reattached thumb. Once fat and full four to six hours later, another hungry leech took its place, a procedure repeated time and again.

"It got to where Isaac started giving the leeches different names," Marian says with a smile. "One was Dr. Rehnke, another was his father and so on."

Toward the end of the week, the Fawcetts became more hopeful that the unique treatment was working, despite the bluish-purple color of Isaac's thumb.

Then, when the doctor carefully removed the layer of dead skin to reveal healthy, pink skin, David Fawcett knew that his prayer he had said for his son the moment after the accident had been answered.

After 10 days in hospital — and about 25 leeches later — Isaac got to go home. And after several weeks of occupational therapy on his thumb, Isaac was on his way to a full recovery, back out in the yard climbing trees and wrestling with his brother, as well as helping his father with the yard work, once again.

"We are so thankful to God, to Dr. Rehnke, to the wonderful nurses at the hospital, to Isaac's occupational therapist Vicki Darlington and to everyone else," Marian adds.

"And when we think about it, modern medicine really is incredible. But it's also pretty neat that God created these little creatures, these 'medicinal snails,' to help out."

Charles Guastella
Columbia St. Petersburg Medical Center
St. Petersburg, Florida

CODE FEAR

Never could anyone ever imagine it happening — a murderous rampage in a busy hospital emergency room. Yet, tragically, it did, on the Labor Day evening of September 2, 1996 at Columbia Chippenham Medical Center in Richmond, Virginia. Fueled by a domestic dispute, two women died and four others, including a 3-year-old boy, were shot and injured.

But that is not the heart of this story.

Instead, it is a story about compassion, love and admiration for an emergency room staff that came together professionally, skillfully and unselfishly to carry out one sole mission — to help others.

And the story is uniquely told in the eloquent, first-person account of Karen Anderson, a 37-year-old nurse, wife and mother of two, who wrote her memories as part of post-stress therapy the hospital offered its staff after that tragic night.

Karen was standing in the pediatric area of the emergency room shortly after 7 p.m. that evening, when in the span of seconds, her mind was slammed into overdrive ...

... I hear gunfire close by. I am afraid. Did I really hear gunfire? I have never heard that before. Where is the shooter? Will I die right here in my own emer-

gency department? Patients and visitors are crying out for help. A child is screaming not far from me. I shove a patient behind a bathroom door before I find my hiding place.

"Code Silver, Emergency Room! Code Silver, Emergency Room!" booms from the paging system. What is Code Silver? I do not know. I know Code Blue. I know Code Red. I do not know Code Silver. A respiratory therapist says it means "Criminal Attack." The gunshots are real. I crouch next to the trash can on a dirty floor in my white scrub pants. I listen as a nearby nurse speaks calmly to a 911 operator to request help. How can an emergency room need 911 assistance? We are 911. And I am an emergency room nurse, so I can handle any crisis, even this. But I am terrified. I am trembling. I am tearful. A hand touches my shoulder as a soft voice tells me I will be okay. I am a nurse. Of course I will be okay.

What is happening? Why am I here? My 12-hour shift ends in a few minutes. Will I go home tonight? I am tired and hungry and want to go home. Where is my family? I want to see my children and husband, right now. Maybe they could come and get me. No. I don't want them here. It is not safe.

Where are the police? I am cold. I am sweating. I am numb all over. I glance towards the emergency exit. I am going to run as fast as I can on the count of three. One. Two. No! I am a nurse. I have to stay here in case they need me. I grab a phone and call our director who does not know I am under a desk this very moment. I say the words "disaster, gunfire in the ER, help us." I look around. Everything is frozen in time. We are all posing for a photograph, but no one is smiling. I wish I was outside. But I am a nurse. I need to be here.

It sounds like it's over, whatever it was. I stand slowly, as other nurses, doctors, patients and visitors do the same. We are in slow motion. Will our legs bear the weight of fear? What do I do? Where do I go? There are cries for help nearby. I take a big breath and run toward the uncertainty. My heart is pounding. My cheeks are flushed and my knees are weak as I reach the eye of the storm. So many voices, so many people, so much to do. Physicians are requesting nurses and emergency equipment in every direction. They want gloves, IV lines, tubes, blood, tape, needles, code carts, catheters, x-rays and on and on.

All of my nursing knowledge has come to challenge me at this very moment. I stare in awe at my co-workers. Several are hurriedly lifting a patient on a stretcher. A nurse is running. A doctor looks concerned. So much activity and so much blood. Blood on gloves, on gowns, on chairs and stretchers and on the floors. But there is a quiet calm to all I see. I must stay calm, too. An elderly patient wanders out of her room. She says, "What is going on, honey? I want to leave." My mind agrees but I escort her back to her room. I tell her, "Everything will be okay. You are safe." I want to believe me.

"The Code Cart is coming," I say loudly, as I push a cart towards a bedside. I have enough strength now to move anything with one finger, or so I feel. I cradle the sweaty head of a patient, a terrified child, "You are safe now," I say. "No one can hurt you anymore." I comfort a friend I find staring into a far-away place. Her eyes tell me what words cannot say. "I know how you feel," I say anyway. "There will be help for us, too. I am here with you now."

Why? Why did this happen? I am angry now. How could anyone violate a place as safe as a hospital? Helpless victims and innocent people damaged by a senseless act of violence. I am consumed by the sadness that fills my heart and soul. Every emotion has been touched.

Later, much later, my nursing tasks are complete for the night. I stand alone and look at my hands, shielded by several pairs of gloves. I take them off, *one pair at a time, realizing each pair "belongs" to a different victim. I begin to cry. I am confused and lost and tired and elated. It is over now.*

A comforting arm leads me away to be with the others. "I understand," a voice says, "everything is going to be all right." Yes. Everything is going to be all right. I am a nurse. There will be another day, another shift and another patient who will need me and my co-workers. Yes, our wounds from the night will heal, for we are the caregivers ...

Karen Anderson was only one of several dozen professionals who pulled together that night to counteract the unbelievable with amazing dedication, talent and perseverance.

And of her co-workers, Karen says she will always be "in awe," just as those on the outside of emergency rooms, everywhere, are in awe of people like Karen — one of the world's countless "caregivers."

Marilyn Tavenner
Columbia Chippenham Medical Center
Richmond, Virginia

THE MOUNTAIN IS CLEAR

In the dark hours before dawn on June 3, 1996, Ricky Price was making the most harrowing trip of his life, heading east on Virginia's Route 64 across the Blue Ridge Mountains. With his wife, Gale, asleep in the back seat, cradling their baby, Luke Hunter Price, Ricky was saying at least a prayer a minute as each long mile passed by.

Only three weeks before, Ricky, 38, and Gale, 30, who had been married eight years, had welcomed their first child into the world. With no major health problems apparent in either mother or child, they had taken Luke home to the tiny community of McCoy, south of Roanoke, to the house they shared with Mark, 13, Ricky's son from a previous marriage. Everything the young family had ever dreamed of seemed to have come true.

"About a week later, Luke seemed a little congested and had a little cough, so I took him to the doctor," explains Gale, a nurse at Columbia Montgomery Regional Hospital where Luke was born. "After Dr. Joe Fisher examined him, he told me Luke's abdomen was swollen. Then he said he wanted to do some blood tests to check Luke's liver."

Back at home that afternoon, Gale waited by the phone for the test results. She knew something was wrong the moment she heard Dr. Fisher's voice on the other end of the line. But even then, the news was much worse than she had ever imagined.

Luke's liver functions were "grossly abnormal," and his condition was so severe, Dr. Fisher already had arranged for a specialist — Dr. James Sutphen at the University of Virginia Health Sciences Center — to examine Luke the very next morning.

"When Ricky got home from work, I couldn't keep from crying when I told him," Gale says. "The words were so hard to say."

With no sleep, Gale and Ricky made the three-hour trip over the mountains to the medical center in Charlottesville the next morning. After a full day of testing, Dr. Sutphen's words sliced right through their hearts — Luke appeared to have a serious metabolic liver disease and his liver did not appear to be functioning well. If tests confirmed that initial diagnosis, their infant son was facing major surgery, perhaps even a liver transplant to survive.

"We went into shock, complete despair, in that cold little exam room with Luke," Gale says.

"When Dr. Sutphen left to give us some privacy, Ricky and I held each other and cried. We felt like we were going to lose our precious baby. It was so hard. Ricky finally said that we were leaving, that we weren't going to listen to anything else they had to say, that we were going to take Luke and go home.

"We were halfway down the hall when a nurse stopped us and talked us into staying long enough to talk to the doctor again. She said it was for Luke's sake, so we did."

Still, despite requests to admit Luke that day for further tests, the Prices refused. Luke had never been to church. They would take him home over the weekend, take him to church Sunday morning and then return with him Monday morning to face whatever they had to face.

That Sunday, June 2, 1996, coincidentally was the annual Homecoming Day at the church attended by Ricky, Gale, Mark, Luke and all of their extended families. During the service, the Prices carried Luke to the altar, presenting him to the congregation for the first time — and the entire congregation responded by circling Luke and his parents with prayers.

Less than 12 hours later, Ricky was steering the car through the darkness up Route 64, with Gale and Luke asleep in the back seat on their way to the health sciences center in Charlottesville. Halfway there, the car neared the tallest climb of the drive, Afton Mountain, which is almost always swathed in fog so thick that permanent lights illuminate the highway, day and night.

Along with his own prayers, Ricky's mind was fresh with the other acts of love and prayers offered in Luke's name by their family members, friends, fellow church members and co-workers.

And at that moment, in the blinding blur of fog hugging Afton Mountain, the unreal happened.

Ricky — though he was driving the car up the mountain — felt like someone opened the passenger door and sat down beside him as a warmth came over him. The feeling was so overwhelming, he looked over just to make sure someone hadn't somehow hopped in.

While he could see nothing with his eyes, he felt a presence of someone by his side. And then, from everywhere and nowhere, a voice said:

"Look up, the mountain is clear now."

Within seconds, the car reached the mountain-top.

When it did, the thick fog suddenly vanished as brilliant sunshine poured from the sky, illuminating everything from the green grass to the tallest tree-tops with crystal clear precision. The warmth, outside and inside the car, wrapped tightly around Ricky.

And without the exact words to explain it, he instinctively knew that a spiritual being had not only cleared the fog from the mountaintop so that he and his family could safely cross — but that the mountain of fear they were facing over Luke's condition would be passable, after all.

Arriving at the medical center on time, Dr. Sutphen oversaw a day-long battery of tests on Luke. Close to 5 p.m., he walked into the room where Ricky and Gale were waiting.

"Dr. Sutphen was shaking his head in disbelief," Gale remembers.

The physician said that he had good news. Luke's liver condition had stabilized and improved — an improvement that was quite miraculous.

"Ricky and I were crying again, but this time with joy, not despair. We told the doctor that a lot of prayers had been said for Luke. He smiled and said, 'Well, someone is praying to the right person.'

"It was so wonderful, I just can't explain in words how Ricky and I felt."

As the weeks and then late fall months of 1996 passed, Luke continued to thrive, his mother says, giving her hope that he is growing strong enough to overcome any liver problems if they were to occur in the future.

To her and her husband, it is "crystal clear" that Luke will survive.

"Whenever people ask us what caused Luke's problems," Gale adds, "we tell them we don't know.

"But what we do know is that God gave us something more than a perfect baby. He also gave us a miracle the moment he told my husband to look up, that the mountain was clear."

Suzanne Nagle
Columbia Montgomery Regional Hospital
Blacksburg, Virginia

100% PURE LOVE

The California sun was dipping down into the white-capped waves of the Pacific Ocean that spring evening more than two decades ago when the two little boys raced toward the bathtub — unusually eager for a good scrub because their parents had promised a trip to the local drive-in movie before bedtime.

"I started running the water as the boys got their clothes off and hopped into the tub," says Glinda Williams Taylor, then 24 and the young mother of Randy Williams, 4, and Daniel Williams, 20 months. "They knew I never let them have the water too deep, so Randy turned it off.

"That moment, I saw they would need another towel, so I stepped out into the hall to get one out of the closet. As I did, I heard a little thump behind me. I thought it was Daniel because whenever he dropped one of his bathtub toys, he was too little to reach for it, so he had a habit of getting out, grabbing the toy and getting back in."

No more than five seconds later, Glinda turned and took a step back into the bathroom. Her instinct that the "thump" had been Daniel getting in and out of the tub was right. But instead of a toy, the toddler had pulled an electric hair dryer into the water — and the current was on.

"There was no sound, but I saw the hair dryer, " Glinda says, her voice still shaking after all the years, "and there were my two little boys. Randy was lying on the bottom of the tub, Daniel was halfway on top of him and both of them were quivering so hard, even though their bodies were rigid. As a mother and a nurse, I knew what was happening immediately."

Glinda jerked Daniel out of the tub, breathed into his mouth and clapped his back. He instantly started breathing and screaming. Dropping him to the floor, Glinda then grabbed Randy.

"I tried starting CPR on him, too, but he was much more rigid than Daniel had been, and I knew it wasn't working," she says. "I jumped up, screaming and running out the front door with Randy in my arms.

"Their father was across the street talking to our neighbor and friend, Gary Durham, an off-duty police officer, and the minute they saw me, they ran all-out toward us."

Glinda remembers Gary taking Randy from her arms, then her memory went blank for two full hours. Though she didn't faint — and doctors remarkably could find no sign that she was exposed to the electricity — the next thing Glinda recalls is being in the hospital, thanking everyone for helping save her two boys.

"I don't know what happened to my memory," she says. "Apparently, when Gary took Randy, he told me to call 911, which I apparently did, and I also got blankets to wrap around the boys.

"Before the ambulance arrived, Gary was able to revive Randy, but we all went on to the local hospital. That's when I realized I didn't remember everything that had happened after I got into the yard with Randy in my arms and Daniel running along beside me. But we were so overjoyed that the boys were okay, nothing else mattered a bit."

While Daniel had no after effects at all, Randy had fleeting ones — each vertebra up and down his spine was bruised from being so rigid, and he was lethargic for several days.

Now, 21 years later, both Randy and Daniel are healthy, happily married men with children of their own. Daniel remembers nothing past family talk about the accident, while Randy still remembers lying in the tub and seeing "sparkles" in the water above him.

And Glinda, now a critical care nurse at Columbia Hospital South in Missouri, is a proud grandmother of three, with thankful memories of that

California evening so long ago.

"People have asked me again and again how I was able to react the way I did," she adds. "All I can say is that I believe it was 100 percent unconditional love, that inner strength a mother gets when she needs to do what needs to be done to help her children.

"It was just 100 percent pure love."

Jill Kleier
Columbia Hospital South
Springfield, Missouri

A SILVER HEART FROM HEAVEN

Sniffles, a little fever and a scratchy throat.

Such were the ingredients of a common cold that took a one-in-a-million leap to trigger an adverse immune system reaction which would come heartbeats away from taking away the life of a young newlywed bride. The fact that she survived — thanks, she believes, in no small part to a silver heart from Heaven — places her name in medical record books.

Mary Haddadi, 23, is only the second person in the United States and only the seventh in the world to have been kept alive by an artificial heart and then recover without a donor heart transplant.

"There were times when I would give up," Mary says, a rich maturity palpable in her otherwise youthful voice. "Once, I even told my family and friends not to waste their prayers on me anymore. Thank goodness they didn't listen to me. They never stopped praying, not for a second.

"Now, I'm just so very, very grateful. I know I have been given another chance to live."

Up until the day she caught the cold in the spring of 1996, Mary had already led an eventful life. In 1981 when she was 6 years old, revolution swept through her native Iran. To ensure the safety of her father, a politician of the old regime, her family sought asylum in the United States, relocating to Colorado's Rocky Mountain suburbs of Denver.

Becoming U.S. citizens, Mary — whose given name of "Mahboobeh" proved too difficult for her new friends to pronounce — lived the life of an all-American girl.

She graduated from high school before heading off to college in California. Then, during her sophomore year, she met businessman Farid Haddadi, also a Iran native who had begun a new life in Colorado. Love quickly followed, and they were married July 29, 1995. Bypassing a honeymoon to buy a house, they moved into their home in Denver's suburb of Westminster that November.

Life could hardly have been sweeter for the newlyweds, with Mary only a year away from earning her bachelor's degree in business, they began their dream of starting a family of their own.

Then, one day in May 1996, Mary caught the cold.

"I was one of those healthy people who rarely ever caught a cold," she says, "and when it first started out, I didn't think a thing about it. Just a month before, I'd had my yearly physical, and I was in excellent health. I weighed 120 pounds, and only to stay in shape, I would walk on the treadmill or take walks with my mother. I had never had any health problems, ever."

But the cold hung on, week after week, growing worse with time.

Mary lost her appetite, completely. While she felt better in the mornings, the "bad cold" raged back with a vengeance every evening. Her temperature soared. Chills racked her from head to toe. Every muscle and bone in her body ached. Breathing was difficult. And despite no more than a bite of food and sip of water, she began vomiting uncontrollably.

"My chills were so bad one night, my family wrapped 20 blankets around me, but I was still shaking," Mary says. "We were all getting very scared."

Over the next few days, Mary grew weaker and sicker to the point she could barely move on her own. Her weight had toppled from 120 to 85 pounds. And her heart began to beat so hard and so rapidly, it bulged up from her chest with every beat.

"It was like you couldn't even imagine it," she says. "My shirt would move up and down. I remember thinking, 'How far can a common cold go?' "

Finally, three weeks after she became ill, a specialist made a new, highly alarming diagnosis.

Mary's bad cold virus had triggered her immune

system to fight back, as it would in any individual. But then — in the one-in-a-million chance that even the top medical experts cannot explain — the antibodies in her immune system went "haywire" and began attacking her heart.

As her heart worked harder to fend off the antibodies, it swelled larger and larger, in turn threatening other vital organs. Fluid began to puddle in her lungs, compromising her ability to breath, and her vomiting was the result of her liver slowly shutting down.

When the diagnosis was made, Mary's heart had swelled — almost triple its normal size — and in essence, she was dying. That's when she was immediately rushed by ambulance to Columbia Presbyterian/St. Luke's Medical Center in downtown Denver.

"The doctors were waiting for me," Mary recalls. "They could tell my condition was very bad. They gave me medicine to try to keep my heart from enlarging any more than it already had and said that in some cases, the virus stops on its own. But the next day, they knew I was getting worse.

"That's when Dr. James Narrod, the cardiac surgeon, came in to talk to me and my family. He was very kind, but he told us the truth."

Mary's chances of survival were low. The only possible remedy was immediate open-heart surgery to connect her to a mechanical heart to allow her own heart a chance to rest and possibly heal. If it failed to heal, a donor heart transplant would be the last resort. And the risks of the surgery to connect her heart to the machines in her current condition were enormous.

There was a one-third chance she would survive, a one-third chance she would remain in heart failure and a one-third chance she would die.

"It was so hard on my family," Mary says. "I had made my husband promise me no surgery, ever, so he kept asking them to wait one more hour, then another hour to see if I didn't start getting better.

"Finally, my brother told him and all my other family members that they had two choices. They could wait and do nothing and watch me die, or my husband could sign for the surgery. My brother said at least then they would know that they had done everything they could to try to save me."

The surgery began at midnight and lasted six and a half hours. Mary awoke in a haze, with the two mechanical heart pumps lying on her stomach and the tube of a ventilator gagging her throat. For 13 days, she laid there, for the most part intentionally medically paralyzed from the neck down.

"It was horrible, horrible, horrible," she says. "I couldn't move or speak. The tube was in my throat for seven of the days. Oh, how I hated that tube! One night, without knowing it, I clamped my teeth down on it, cutting off all the oxygen, so I stopped breathing. I don't remember it, but they had to give me two shots real quick into the nerves behind my ears to make my jaw pop open.

"And the heart pumps were so heavy and so loud, I could hardly even escape into sleep. I didn't know how much more I could take. Sometimes, I just gave up."

Unknown to Mary, the severity of her condition led her doctors to encourage her family members and friends to gather at the hospital for a last visit. Her name had also risen to the top of the list for persons in most dire need of a donor for a heart transplant.

Her family and friends who gathered — including her mother who spent virtually 24 hours a day at Mary's bedside — decided that no matter how difficult it was on them, they would not shed a tear in front of Mary. They didn't want to risk weakening her spirit by letting her know how close she was to death.

Outside her room was a different story. Family and friends from as far away as Switzerland began arriving at the hospital. And on one particular afternoon, they persuaded Mary's mother to make a quick trip home to freshen up while they stood vigil at Mary's bedside.

"On her way outside, my mother was crying and praying to God to please help me, to let my heart get back to normal so I could live," Mary says. "Right then, something nicked mother's leg, but she was so upset she didn't even look down or stop.

"But a few seconds later, she had the thought that somebody else might get hurt by whatever hit her leg, so she turned around and walked back.

"That's when she saw it, a silver heart lying on the street. It was a silver picture frame, about the size of a plate, shaped like a heart. Everything was gone but the metal frame. It was so amazing that she stumbled over it.

"She said she picked it up and screamed a thank you to God. She said she knew then that He was going to answer her prayers."

Running back up to Mary's room, her mother brought in the silver heart and excitedly whispered,

"You are going to be fine! You're heart is going to be fine! God gave me this to tell me all our prayers will be answered!"

Mary underwent two more open-heart surgeries to remove the artificial hearts. After 45 days in intensive care, she was moved to her own room at the hospital. And a week later, she was released.

"It wasn't until then that everybody told me how sick I had been," Mary adds. "Dr. Narrod told me if they hadn't operated when they did, my heart would have stopped working within 24 hours.

"Now, all the doctors, all the nurses, my family and friends and all of their prayers have given me a new chance at life. Every bit of my story is amazing to me, especially because I am so very fortunate to have so many people love me."

Mary is expected to live a long, full life with the ability to do all the things she once dreamed. She plans to return to college in 1997 to earn her degree. A few years from now, she and her husband hope to have children if her heart is strong enough, or through adoption.

And from her experience, Mary has also found a new dream.

During her long hospital stay, she noticed that

while she had more visitors than the doctors would often allow, many other patients faced their own illnesses alone.

That's why she has decided to become a volunteer at Columbia St. Luke's, just to chat with lonely patients, hold their hand if they want and if they are frightened, she'll tell them a story about a common cold and a silver heart from Heaven.

Danielle Perry
Columbia Presbyterian/St. Luke's Medical Center
Denver, Colorado

DAZEE DING DONG

Forget dancing elephants, daring high-wire antics, roaring lions jumping through fiery hoops or loud horns screeching beep-beep.

One very special clown — Dazee Ding Dong — prefers a much softer approach.

"She is the most gentle person you will ever meet," says Marge Vita, director of volunteer services at Columbia Blake Medical Center in Bradenton, Florida. "She's not a boisterous clown. She's very laid back. People, both the patients and the staff, just naturally respond to her and reach out to her, as well.

"She's just wonderful."

Dazee Ding Dong — otherwise known as 66-year-old retiree Jule McRae — is a trained volunteer "clinical clown" at the medical center. And her only "act," which she obviously adores, is to add a little bit of laughter and happiness to patients young and old during their hospital stay.

"She's like the cream in the coffee, the icing on the cake," Marge explains. "We give great care here at the hospital, but these are little touches that make a difference. She's just perfect at what she does."

Jule became interested in "clinical clowning" in the 1980s after hearing about the concept through a church group in Ohio. The idea captivated her, so over the years she took a number of training classes before bringing her "act" to Florida when she and her husband moved south after retirement in the early 1990s.

When attired in her floppy hat and smiling make-up, Dazee has a range of talents that would impress even the most experienced big-tent circus clowns.

Along with her laughter, she can weave wonderful stories, speak in sign language, put on a puppet show and has the ability to "read between the fears or tears" of the patients.

That was proven one afternoon when the hospital staff was growing increasingly concerned about an elderly patient who had neither said a word nor eaten since she had been admitted a day or so before. Despite endless pleas from doctors and nurses, the condition of the woman grew more and more precarious.

Then Dazee happened by her room

A nurse's aide was trying to get the woman to sip some soup when Dazee — in her quiet, gentle style — breezed in. The aide looked up at her with pleading eyes.

With her big, bright, painted-on smile spread even wider by a smile of her own, Dazee edged over to the bedside, looked down at the frail woman and quietly said, "Hello."

After surveying her unusual, colorfully dressed, fanciful visitor, a hint of recognition shined in the woman's eyes.

"Hello," the woman managed to say, weakly.

Astonished, the nurse's aide scrambled to make the most of the moment by offering her patient another spoonful of soup. Dazee, ever sensitive to the patients and the staff, went on talking in her mild-mannered way as the woman swallowed spoonful after spoonful of warm soup. And from that one encounter, the woman began talking to everyone — and eating, allowing her condition to improve.

"That's just one of many happy endings that begin with a visit from Dazee Ding Dong," Marge says.

"She brings in sunshine and much more. There's a sense of love, of charity about her, the kind of charity that's a connotation of love."

As she makes her "rounds" at the medical center, Dazee carries a variety of stickers for patients, employees and visitors, alike.

"Hurrah for You!" reads one.

"I Think You're Super!" reads another.

She also has her very own, very special "prescription" pad.

Unlike most doctors' prescriptions, Dazee's are highly legible and direct. Some of her typical prescriptions include:

"Three hugs once a day."

"Five smiles an hour."

"Six new handshakes a week."

"Dazee passes them out to everyone," Marge says with a chuckle. "Whenever she's here, there's no mistaking that she's around. You can't miss Dazee, her laughter and her love for everyone here."

Beyond her visits to the medical center, Dazee also puts her love and enthusiasm to work by teaching courses on how to become a "clinical clown."

That way, Jule McRae passes on the secret of Dazee Ding Dong — how a simple, gentle smile can often make all the difference in the world.

Marge Vita
Columbia Blake Medical Center
Bradenton, Florida

IN SWADDLING CLOTHES

As the couple walked into the hospital, each slow step seemed dreaded, a look which matched the gaze in their eyes.

It was March 1996 in Lafayette, Louisiana, and the man and woman — only 24 weeks into her pregnancy — knew their baby had died in her womb. They had come to Columbia Women & Children's Hospital to deliver a stillborn son. All they could expect to be taking home were tattered memories of a life they created which would never take a breath in this world.

While nothing could be done to stop their pain, they would soon find that because of one woman's idea and a group of caring strangers, their despair would be slightly lightened by a tiny slip of cloth, an inch or two of lace and several tiny buttons.

"To a mother and father, nothing can compare to the loss of a child," says Mary Broussard, director of social services at Columbia Women's & Children's Hospital.

"And for parents who lose a son or daughter before or shortly after birth, the pain takes on another cruel twist. They often never have the chance to see their infant dressed in beautiful baby clothes before they have to say good-bye."

Such was the genesis of Mary's idea.

And the happily married mother of five children — aged 16, 14, 12, 10 and 8 — had known exactly what to say in January 1995 when she received a call from the Louisiana Bayou Chapter of the Smocking Arts Guild of America.

"They wanted to know what they could do to help, and I immediately thought of the families who lost babies so early," Mary says.

"While we've always done our best to help in their bereavement, I thought how wonderful it would be if we had clothes small enough to fit the infants who never made it into this world alive, or those little ones who died very soon after they were born.

"The smocking guild took the idea and ran with it. Within weeks, they were sending us these wonderful, handmade gowns small enough to dress these tiny infants so that their mothers and fathers could see their babies wearing a baby gown, at least one time."

The response was immediate and heartfelt.

"Everything kind of blossomed," Mary says. "With the gowns, we were able to tastefully photograph the baby to give their parents a keepsake. And clothed so beautifully, the babies often take on the appearance that they are sleeping peacefully.

"We soon learned how meaningful it is for these

mothers and fathers to be able to see their child wearing a pastel baby gown, rather than a plain, hospital baby blanket. And for us, we knew we were doing something positive to help the parents take the first step in their long grieving process."

But it wasn't until a few weeks after the couple delivered their stillborn son in March 1996 that Mary and her staff discovered the truly invaluable worth of the smocking guild's gifts.

"It had only been two weeks, so I remembered the woman very well," Mary says. "After she gave birth to the baby boy, we dressed him in one of the gowns and took him into the room with his parents. Both of them had cried softly as they cradled their lifeless son, stroked his face and held his miniature hands in theirs.

"Before they left the hospital, they had told us that they would hold the memory of that moment as a treasure to carry with them, forever.

"Then, after two weeks, the mother had come back to visit us."

Going through the labor and delivery unit to thank everyone who had helped her and her husband, she then walked into Mary's office.

"She told me again how much it had meant to them to have that time with their son, "Mary says, "then as she got up to leave, she handed me a bag."

Inside, Mary saw a swath of soft, baby blue fabric, matching thread, a spool of lacy ribbon and a packet of tiny, heart-shaped buttons.

As the woman walked out, she told Mary that she wanted the smocking guild to have the materials to make more gowns for babies like her son.

"I was astonished," Mary says. "Here was a mother who had just lost her baby and, despite her own grief, she wanted to do something to help other mothers and fathers who found themselves sharing the same pain."

Mary humbly accepted the gift.

She says the encounter etched in stone the fact that swaddling clothes surely do lighten, at least a little, the heavy hearts of parents who lose a child so early.

While their lives will never be the same, compassionate and caring communities and caregivers offer a circle of support — and allow the parents to remember their children wearing pastel pink or blue gowns, reflecting the first rainbow rays of sunrise which flow down each morning from the heavens.

Jill Bayless
Columbia Women's & Children's Hospital
Lafayette, Louisiana

MAGIC POTION

Without warning, a time bomb began counting down the moment Kim Wenda walked into her best friend's living room on the night of May 6, 1995.

Though she had no way to know it then, the next 96 hours would become the most critical four days of Kim's life — though the days should have been some of the happiest.

At 31, Kim and her husband Mark, 34, after being married seven years, had just discovered they were going to have their first child.

That was the news they were delivering to their friends on their visit that night.

"We were all so excited," Kim says. "My best friend was thrilled for us, and her two little girls were, too. They were crawling all over Mark and me, giggling about the new playmate they would have in about nine months.

"It was a fabulous night."

Twenty four hours later, Kim and Mark were in their own home in the central Illinois town of Petersburg, packing their suitcases for a long-planned Florida vacation to her parent's condo in Naples when the telephone rang.

"It was my best friend asking me if I'd ever had the chicken pox," Kim says. "I wasn't sure what she was talking about at first, but I told her no, that I was probably the only kid in my elementary school who hadn't caught them.

"When I asked her why, she said she suspected her girls may have caught them from a friend, so I had better call my doctor. I'd heard how dangerous it can be for pregnant women to be exposed to the measles, but I'd never heard that about chicken pox.

"Still, Mark and I had waited a long time to have a baby. We didn't want to take any chances."

Kim immediately dialed her doctor's call service.

When he called her back, he said she probably didn't have anything to worry about but to call him from Florida if her friend found out for sure that her daughters were indeed infected. In that case, he told Kim she would need to get a shot since it can be extremely risky for expectant mothers who had not had chicken pox when they were young to catch the virus, especially in the early months of pregnancy.

Those risks could run the full range from the possibility of a miscarriage to severe deformity. But the medication would counteract the virus, he said, whisking away the risks.

"It was kinda scary, but the doctor said all I would need was a shot if the girls happened to have chicken pox," Kim recalls. "But he did tell me to be prepared because the shot would be very expensive, about $1,000.

"I could hardly believe that, but I didn't worry too much about it at the time because the doctor didn't seem all that concerned. So the next morning, we flew on down to Florida."

Forty-eight hours after playing with the two little girls, Kim called her girlfriend from the beach-front condo. A visit to their pediatrician had confirmed that the girls did indeed have chicken pox.

"Of course I was concerned, but when I called my doctor, he told me to calm down," Kim says. "He said all I needed to do was relax and call the local pharmacies until I found one that had the drug I needed for the shot.

"He told me the big long name of the medicine and said to call him when I found someone who had it in stock."

It was a restless day for Kim and Mark, with the necessity for the drug — and its ungainly long name of "Varicella Zoster Immuneglobulin" — attacking their vacation.

Shortly after the doctor's phone call, Kim looked at the clock and counted the hours since she had been exposed. Roughly 36 hours remained in the time window in which she must have the shot in order for it to be effective.

She opened the yellow pages to the pharmacy section. And with Mark by her side, she began dialing the numbers.

"I called and called and called at least 15 of them," Kim says. "Some of them were nice, apologizing that they didn't have it. Others said they'd never even heard of it, without offering more help.

"I was getting more and more upset with every call. I couldn't help it. I mean, there we were in a strange town, I couldn't even pronounce the name of the drug I knew I had to find to keep our baby safe and no one would help us.

"Getting nowhere, I finally called my doctor back to tell him what was going on. That's when he told me I must get the shot and that I must get it within the 96-hour time frame. He said for me to try calling the pharmacies at the local hospitals, that surely they would have it."

Kim dialed the three local hospitals. None had the medicine she needed.

"That's when bad went to terrible for us," she says. "I broke down crying and everything, and Mark was just as upset, worrying about me and us finding the drug.

"We were running out of time and didn't know

what to do."

Frantically flipping through the phone book in search of anyone, anywhere who might help, Kim came across a listing for Columbia Healthcare Referral/The Professionals in nearby Fort Myers. She desperately punched in the number.

"I was hysterical by the time a registered nurse with the service named Susan Bills got on the line," Kim says. "I don't know how she ever even understood my babbling. I kept telling her over and over that I had to find this stuff.

"Susan was so gentle. She said, 'Calm down. I will find it for you. I will do all the hunting. You just settle down and call me back.'

"I was still crying, but no one, not even Susan, will ever understand how much her words and her promise meant to me and Mark that moment."

The nervous afternoon hours slipped away — dipping down ever closer to the 24-hour-mark in which Kim had to have the injection. Taking Susan's suggestion, Kim and Mark went for a ride, trying to pull themselves together and "have fun" before the appointed time to call Susan back arrived.

In the meantime, Susan went into high gear, making numerous calls to area physicians, trying to track down the medication. Finally, an infectious disease specialist suggested she contact the Red Cross. Calling the local Fort Myers office, she was referred to the Red Cross affiliate in Daytona Beach, more than a hundred miles to the north.

"We could hardly believe it when we called Susan back and she told us she'd located the medicine," Kim recalls. "That was the first ray of hope we'd had since the whole nightmare began.

"But the three of us didn't know then that we still had a long way to go on the crazy roller-coaster ride we were on."

The first hurdle was getting the medicine — priced at $996 — to the Naples area. At one point, Kim and Mark were preparing to drive northward to pick it up, but Susan managed to have it flown in the next day on a flight scheduled to arrive at 3 p.m. — four hours before the 96-hour time frame came to an end.

The next obstacle was finding a physician in the area to agree to give Kim the injection.

Once again, Susan was the link in getting Kim's physician in Illinois to overnight her records to a family practitioner in Florida who then had to follow the standard rules of examining Kim before administering the drug.

"Mark and I were at the doctor's office the next

afternoon right at 3:30 when the medicine was supposed to arrive," Kim says. "We were standing there in the waiting room next to the receptionist's counter when the telephone rang. We heard her say, 'Yes, they're right here.'

"Our hearts sank looking at the expression on her face. After everything we'd gone through, we couldn't imagine what might have gone wrong. When she hung up, she told us real softly that the plane was late.

"It was so emotional. All we could do was wait."

At 5 p.m. — with barely two hours to spare — three tiny vials of medicine packed in a huge box arrived at the doctor's office, and Kim, at last, received the dosage she needed to guard the safety of the baby she was carrying.

After "trying" to vacation for the remaining five days, Kim and Mark returned home, never having a chance to meet Susan or many of the other people Susan persuaded to help.

Then, on November 6, 1995, Nathanial Steven Wenda, "Nate" to his family and friends, came "screaming up a storm into the world, as happy and as healthy as could be," according to his mother.

In the months before and after his birth, many grateful notes of thanks and then baby pictures were mailed to nurse Susan Bills in Florida.

And Kim says now that she can hardly wait for the day when Nate is old enough to hear about his "guardian angel."

"I totally love her," Kim adds. "I know in my heart that without Susan, I would never have gotten the medicine I had to have in order to have a perfect, wonderful, healthy baby.

"I also know how extraordinary it was for a stranger to step in that role by going out of her way, not just by one but by countless extra miles, to make sure an unborn baby would one day have a life to live.

"And when I tell my family and friends about our 'guardian angel,' I make sure to tell them that in addition to the angels in Heaven, there's a few right here on Earth. One of them is named Susan."

Greg Benefiel
Columbia Healthcare Referral
Fort Myers, Florida

GOD'S GOLD CHAIN REACTION

Winter slashed through the southern United States in the early months of 1994 with a ravenously wild rage. Temperatures tumbled. Savage winds swirled. And ice shot down from the heavy clouds, encasing everything with its clear cement.

It was one of the worst winters on record, claiming a number of lives and causing millions of dollars in damage.

Yet, in keeping with nature's plan, spring brought a warm breeze to breathe life into budding yellow buttercups, then summer brought its steamy hot air to ripen green tomatoes and welcome the southern states back into a more familiar routine.

That only left the lengthy clean-up of the ice storms. It was a mammoth task, one which Marc Collins, 22, found himself a part of on the afternoon of August 2, 1994.

As a lineman for the rural electric company which serves the area near his home in the sleepy Arkansas community near Hamburg, Marc and his fellow workers were chopping down some of the last ice-shattered branches to completely clear the electrical lines.

"I remember we were cutting trees," Marc says, "and I remember climbing up the pole to take the line down. Then, I turned to put the wire back, and that's the last thing I remember."

But his co-workers remember everything that happened next, vividly.

Marc was atop the towering pole — 34 feet in the air and secured in that position by his spike-toed shoes and by holding a guy wire in his left hand.

That's when a "live" wire accidentally slipped down, brushing the top of his head.

The full force of 7,620 volts of electricity — easily 76 times more fiery energy than necessary to kill a man — zapped down through his skull.

And, like a lifeless, scorched mannequin, Marc instantly fell the 34 feet to the ground.

As his co-workers watched him fall, their thoughts switched into slow motion, thinking of Marc. A football player and graduate of the local high school, he'd been on the job just over three years. He was a good kid who always had one-liners to bring them out of the doldrums on long workdays, or make an okay workday a little more fun with his laid-back, lighthearted manner. And when he wasn't at work, Marc was either helping his mother, out hunting ducks or at the rodeo, charming the crowds with his thrillingly comical clown maneuvers as a red-flag swinging "bullfighter." All in all, he was the kind of guy with a knack for making life a little bit better whenever he was around.

Those thoughts of Marc were quickly followed by silent prayers as the workers rushed him to the closest hospital in nearby Greenville, Mississippi.

For seven days, Marc lay unconscious on the edge of death, attached to life only by a ventilator and other high-tech medical machines. Doctors were amazed he had survived the monstrous shock and the incredible fall, and their amazement continued as Marc held on, day after day.

After a week passed, his condition had stabilized. But the doctors there knew more sophisticated medical treatments would be required if Marc was to have any real shot to survive.

With the help of a case nurse, arrangements were made to airlift Marc several hundred miles away to Columbia Doctor's Hospital in Little Rock.

Once the medical helicopter landed and the Little Rock doctors examined him, they, too, were amazed Marc had survived — thanks to a pair of Ray-Ban sunglasses and an 18-inch, solid gold rope chain necklace he had been wearing the moment of the accident.

"When I finally woke up in Little Rock," Marc says, with his ever-present chuckle, "the doctors told me I was awful lucky. And when they told me what had happened, I didn't have much choice but to agree with them."

He knew that the nature of electricity is to race along the quickest path of least resistance — and gold is one of its favorite runways.

So when the huge jolt of current entered the top of his head, it instantly gravitated to the metal frames of his sunglasses — severely burning the skin where the rims touched his face beneath his eyes — but the leap of current to the metal saved him from certain blindness.

Second, as the current found the gold chain around his neck, it immediately melted it — the bubbling gold digging down to critically burn the skin beneath it — yet saving his life by virtually cutting off the current to the rest of his body.

"Considering all that and falling 34 feet," Marc laughs, "you gotta figure I am pretty lucky."

Marc's extraordinary attitude remained in full swing, never faltering even when it became apparent that his left hand — which had been holding the guy wire when the accident occurred and subsequently had been horribly burned — would have to be amputated several inches above his wrist.

"All right," he told his nurse, Kay Saunders, "do

what you need to do, but just make sure my Mama's okay."

When asked how he remained so upbeat, he simply declared, "I just didn't care to get depressed, so I didn't."

During the next month, Marc underwent the amputation, several other surgeries and therapy treatments before he was finally ready to go home.

After "getting to know" his new prosthetic left hand, Marc was back climbing electric poles six months later — waiting on purpose, he says, for duck hunting season to end before returning to work.

In the two years which have passed since the accident, Marc is busier than ever. During his months of recovery, he took up the hobby of raising bob-white quails — four or five thousand of them — and he's also been frequently called upon to return to the hospital in Little Rock, not for treatment for him, but to share his sky-high spirits with new amputees.

"I didn't have a clue what to say the first couple of times I drove up there," he says, "but I figured it out pretty quick.

"I tell the patients this right up front. 'If you just take a look around this old world, there's a whole lot of people a whole lot worse off than you are. You gotta go on 'cause this isn't the end of the world.'

"It may take them a little while to get used to it, but that's the truth."

One glance at Marc's life now makes that point as clear as the ice that fell on the south during the winter of 1994.

He has not allowed the accident to alter his lifestyle "one iota."

"Okay, it's like this," he says, in between belly laughs. "I got me a permanent necklace scar around my neck, I got me a new hand and I still do everything I did before. It was just something that happened."

And while many people — with medical experts topping the list — say that Marc's survival was miraculous, he shrugs that kind of talk off in his down-home, forever optimistic way.

"All the talk about a miracle and a gold chain and stuff like that sounds good," he says, with a big smile.

"But if you ask me, the fact of the matter is that the good Lord just didn't want me right then."

Kay Saunders
Columbia Doctor's Hospital
Little Rock, Arkansas

SLEEPING BEAUTY

A crisp chill rippled through the autumn air as the sun began to rise over western Tennessee on September 8, 1995, wonderful weather for an early morning run.

So the attractive young woman with long, blonde hair quickly got out of bed, pulled on a pair of pink shorts and a gray sweatshirt and set off on a brisk sprint around the streets of Jackson, the largest city between Memphis and Nashville.

"A passing motorist noticed her easy stride and relaxed run," says Karolyn Henry, director of public relations at Columbia Regional Hospital of Jackson. "Right at that last moment, she was so healthy and alive."

Less than 30 seconds later, a speeding pickup truck rounded a curve, slid off the road and struck the young runner.

On impact, she was thrown 25 yards into the air before crashing back down onto the ground. The bone in her right leg snapped. A rib was cracked. Her kidney was internally torn. But the most ferocious force thrashed her head and neck as her body sprawled motionless, her long hair tangled with twigs, grass and mud.

In spite of her violent internal injuries, the only

outward sign of trauma was a single cut on her face, from her hairline to her right eyebrow.

Sirens soon screamed through the autumn air to transport the young woman by ambulance the two short minutes away to the emergency room at Columbia Regional Hospital of Jackson.

Once there, she lay comatose as nurses cut away her tattered clothing though finding no identification, as physicians specializing in orthopedics, neurology, urology and internal medicine answered their urgent pages, arriving at the hospital.

While the young woman was ushered through countless rounds of examinations, x-rays and other medical tests, word flew through the hospital like wildfire that a beautiful "Jane Doe" was in critical condition in the emergency room, words which ignited a wave of prayers.

To the physicians and staff close enough to see her, "Jane Doe" reminded them of a "Sleeping Beauty," though they knew she needed more than a kiss to be awakened — and a miracle to survive.

"Since she was the age of a college student and was near the school when she was struck, someone in our hospital administration office called nearby Union University to ask if the young woman could be a missing student," Karolyn says.

"None had been reported. But the president of the private, religious university appeared at the morning chapel program, telling the students about the accident and then asking them to look around the 1,200-seat chapel to make sure all their roommates and suite-mates were there.

"Three girls came forward to report that their newest suite-mate, a runner with long, blonde hair who had transferred from Florida Bible College to the university only 10 days before, was nowhere to be seen.

"Her name was Amy Elizabeth Edwards."

A second wave of prayers rose from the university chapel for the young woman few people knew, while school officials scampered to contact Amy's family in Taylors, South Carolina.

Soon, her mother, Marge Edwards, was on a plane to Memphis. At the same time, Amy's two sisters and a brother-in-law picked up their father, Jock Edwards, and began the 10-hour drive to Tennessee, while Amy's brother and his wife left their Atlanta home for Jackson.

Back at the hospital, the staff automatically adopted Amy as their own, with many of the professionals and staff support members thinking of their own children and realizing — through their "Sleeping Beauty" — how quickly life can change.

In the Radiology Department, the director talked to Amy, urging her to open her eyes and talk as she underwent a CT scan to determine the extent of brain and spinal injuries. One specialist overheard the director and sadly remarked that Amy probably would never open her eyes or speak again.

Later, laboratory workers were elated when they thought Amy squeezed their hands as they drew blood from her arm, but a physician gently told them the squeeze was most likely no more than a reflex motion.

Still, as the critical care nurses prepared a room for Amy, hushed voices throughout the hospital asked, "How's Amy? Is anything new?"

In those first hours, Amy underwent several immediate procedures. The cut on her face was stitched together and her leg was placed in traction.

By the time her mother arrived at the hospital, Amy's friends in South Carolina and others from her former college campus in Florida had joined in the chorus of prayers for her recovery, while members of Jackson area churches joined in with prayers and offerings of food and other necessities to comfort Amy's family members.

Twelve days later on September 20, it became clear that surgery to place a steel rod in her broken leg was necessary, along with a tracheostomy to help her breathing.

"It was a difficult decision for us to sign for surgery," her mother says. "We knew it was needed, but with Amy still in a coma, the thought of her undergoing anesthesia, too, was frightening to us.

"But we knew Amy was in God's hands, so we signed for the surgery and prayed we'd made the right decision."

The surgery went well, and then a team of specialists from a rehabilitation center in Atlanta evaluated her condition and offered hope that they could awaken Amy, over time. So 21 days after the accident, Amy was taken by air-ambulance to Atlanta.

Her departure was met with tearful good-byes and prayers for her recovery among the Jackson hospital staff, along with everyone else in the west Tennessee town who had taken Amy into their hearts. And then as the days, weeks and months passed, everyone eagerly awaited the regular reports from Amy's parents of her slow but steady recovery.

After seven weeks in Atlanta, Amy was transported from Georgia to a rehabilitation hospital in Greenville, South Carolina, only a few miles from her home. It was January 1996, four months since her accident, before Amy began to truly communicate. And through the spring and summer, her progress continued on.

One of her family's fears was how the accident might have affected Amy's memory — particularly her strong relationship with God. Their worries were unneeded.

When Amy was able to speak again, she could still quote the Bible, by heart. She also wrote a "prayer list" during her stay at the Greenville hospital.

"Dear God, this is what I want," it read in part. "To be able to walk again, to talk well, to stop my shaking, to hear well, to live with my family at home, to write again, to drink through a straw, to have a normal brain that isn't hurt, to be able to put on makeup again and, one day, I want to get married."

Her mother says Amy's prayer list "let us know she was truly emerging and that she was aware of her limitations."

At the same time, Marge says that Amy wrote a

"thank you list to God" which included things such as being thankful for her family, her wheelchair and walker — even though she didn't like the fact she had to use them — the video camera "to help me see how I am improving" and the piano she "wished I could play."

"We knew then and still know that Amy is in God's hands," Marge explains. "He definitely has a plan for her, and it is God who gives her the will to live and the determination to work hard, everyday, to improve."

Amy made more headway through the summer and early fall of 1996. She worked hard to be independent in the wheelchair and continued her struggle to walk with the walker. She also fought to regain her abilities to write, play the piano and swim. She tackled all these challenges without the ability to hear — a problem discovered in January, though she learned to deal with it by reading lips, interpreting charades and easily reading written messages from her family, friends and therapists.

All in all, Amy battles daily for life as she once knew it. And despite the hardships along that journey, her mother says that Amy has a glow about her that can only be explained by an inner strength from

God.

And Amy made a definite date — to return to Columbia Regional Hospital of Jackson on September 8, 1996 — the first anniversary of the day she arrived in her injury-tattered pink shorts and gray sweatshirt. She wanted to thank the staff for saving her life — and the staff was more than eager to see "Sleeping Beauty" awake and alive. And most important to Amy, she wanted to show them her progress by walking into the hospital.

As her family wheeled her to the front hospital doors that anniversary day, Amy was amazed to see dozens of staff members and health care professionals lining the main entrance and front lobby in anticipation of her visit. The crowd collectively held their breath as they watched Amy rise from her wheelchair and, with the help of a walker, slowly make her way inside.

The moment she stepped across the threshold on her own power and raised her head to beam a beautiful smile to everyone, a thunderous applause stampeded through the hospital — a sound so loud that Amy could hear it, despite her hearing loss.

"We were thrilled with her recovery to that point," Karolyn says, tears brimming in her eyes, "and we still have plenty of prayers left for her continued success.

"Amy has already come through so much that we know she has already beaten the odds. She's our 'Sleeping Beauty' who is now wide awake and on her way to full and happy life.

"That's the miracle we all asked God for, a miracle that still goes on for Amy."

Karolyn Henry

Columbia Regional Hospital of Jackson
Jackson, Tennessee

HEAVENLY HINTS

Sunshine waltzed like gold glitter across the Great Salt Lake in northern Utah on the warm Wednesday morning of August 21, 1996.

Only a short sprint away on the football field at Ogden High School, Coach James Price was directing a practice session of passes, punts, tackles and game plans his team of young athletes would blend into the fall football season in their quest for touchdowns and extra points.

All the rough and tumble plays were going well when right at 10 a.m., one of the new freshman running backs, Daniel Cho, 15, walked over to the coach and said he felt dizzy. Knowing football knocks can make anyone a little shaky, Coach Price told him to take a break. Daniel obeyed, standing next to the coach.

Then, about five minutes later without voicing further complaints, Daniel collapsed to the ground. Ed Carlisle, the team's trainer, rushed over and both he and the coach quickly realized that whatever was happening was serious.

Daniel was unconscious.

Using a cellular phone kept at the field, the trainer rapidly dialed 911. Then he had someone call Daniel's mother to ask if the boy had any special medical problems they were unaware of, as well as urge her to quickly come to the school.

A Korean native, Daniel's mother Sooja — "Sue" to her American friends since her family emigrated here in 1991 — answered with alarm, explaining that her son was in excellent health to her knowledge, before running to her car for the short drive to the high school.

Within five minutes of the 911 call, paramedics were on the field. Sue was there moments later.

"They were bringing him on a stretcher to the ambulance," she says. "To me, he first looked like there was no problem. He looked like he was sleeping. But when I called his name, he didn't respond.

"I knew then it was very bad. To me, everything turned into a bad dream. I could not believe this thing was happening. I felt empty, so empty."

As the ambulance screeched away toward Columbia Ogden Regional Medical Center, school principal Larry Leatham helped Sue into his car and they closely followed behind.

From the ambulance, the paramedics radioed in to alert the staff that they were transporting a head trauma victim. A nurse immediately passed the alert on to a neurosurgeon, so he could be prepared in the event brain surgery was needed.

The minute Daniel arrived at the emergency room at 10:40 a.m., he was dashed into the radiology department for a CT scan of his brain. It confirmed the frightening fears.

During football practice, Daniel's head had received a blow hard enough to cause a large subdural hematoma — a localized swelling resulting from broken blood vessels.

For Daniel to live, emergency brain surgery was essential.

And at 11:07 a.m., one hour and two minutes after he slumped to the grassy football field, Daniel was in surgery.

Down the hallway, his mother — with no family members available to comfort her — waited with the school principal, the hospital chaplain, a social worker and the bishop of her church.

"I was crying so much," Sue says. "I was so sad and upset, I could not think. I could not even pray hard like I wanted to. The people around me were very nice. They said everything would be all right. But I was crying so much."

Later, with the surgery completed, Sue remembers the doctor walking toward them.

"The principal asked the doctor how was Daniel," she explains. "The doctor said if the number one was good and the number five was bad, Daniel was a four. He said it was now up to Daniel.

"If Daniel would respond in 24 hours, then he had a hope. If he did not respond, he did not have a hope."

Sue says she cannot find words — in English or her native Korean dialect— to explain how she felt at that moment.

But then, with the circle of friends praying around her, she found the courage to pray — very hard.

"I asked the Heavenly Father not to take my Daniel away from me," she says softly.

And that moment, Sue says, she knew her prayer would be answered.

"I felt very warm, very quiet and very calm, like faith was all around me," she says. "I knew the Heavenly Father was not going to take Daniel away. I knew for a fact that Daniel would be well again."

The "warmth of faith" silenced her tears, Sue says, and "put a calm inside my heart."

Within 24 hours, Daniel began to respond, slowly opening his eyes. And on Friday, two days after the emergency surgery, he was fully awake.

In the time which has passed since then, his recuperation has been slow — but distinctly steady. He can speak clearly, walk with the help of a cane and has returned to high school classes on a limited schedule.

And most importantly, doctors believe Daniel will be completely healed, as if the accident never happened.

But Daniel, who has no memory of his early days in the hospital, knows that the accident did indeed happen — and for a reason.

"Daniel believes the accident was the Heavenly Father's way of trying to teach him a lesson or give him a hint about something," his mother says. "Now, he does not know for sure what it is about.

"But when we were talking, I told him to remember how he said he wanted to be a doctor long before the accident. I told him that now, if he does become a doctor, he will know the feelings of people who get hurt and he can help them better, knowing how they feel."

Daniel likes to think that is the hint God was giving him.

And Sue is certain the warm feeling of faith she

felt moments after Daniel's surgery was a direct hint from God that Daniel would recover.

"I knew my son would be all right," she adds. "The Heavenly Father let me know He wanted it that way."

Sister Stephanie Mongeon
Columbia Ogden Regional Medical Center
Ogden, Utah

VIPER VICTORY

He never heard a rattle.

He never saw the snake make a lightning fast strike.

Instead, the six-foot long Canebrake rattlesnake lazily opened its mouth and sunk one fang into the top of Gary Waller's left hand, just above his thumb.

"I can picture that moment in my mind as if it happened a second ago," says Gary, 34, an electrician for the local Lufkin Independent School District near his Texas home where he kept a collection of native snakes.

"My first thought was, 'Well, he got me.' Then I put him up, walked in the house and told my wife to get the keys because we were going to the hospital."

Growing up in a rugged region where rattlesnakes are as much a part of the fertile lowlands as golden-rods and hackberry trees, Gary's fascination and respect for the lethal reptiles stretched back to his teenage days. For almost 20 years, he had collected snakes from the wild, caring for them as dazzling, though dangerous pets.

Never once had they posed a threat before that Monday afternoon of February 19, 1996, when Gary took the rattler out of its cage so that his nephews and cousin could capture it with their camera lens for a school project.

It was then, in a fraction of a second, that one of the rattlesnake's needle-sharp fangs had injected a huge dose of deadly venom directly into Gary's bloodstream.

"It didn't hurt a bit," he says, "no tingling feeling, nothing. But I knew he'd gotten me. After I put him up, I looked for the snake bite kit I always take with me whenever I go hunting, but I couldn't find it. That's when I told my wife that we'd better get on to the hospital."

Twenty minutes later, Gary was inside the emergency room of Columbia Woodlands Heights Medical Center in Lufkin.

"I was sitting there when it hit me," he says. "They were taking my vital signs when I told them I was about to get sick. The last thing I remember is my tongue swelling so big I couldn't breathe."

Before passing out, Gary managed to tell the staff that the bite came from a Canebrake rattler — vital information since to be effective, any antivenin that could save his life had to match the type of venom in his system. So, as the poison hurled Gary into unconsciousness and coursed its way through his veins and arteries, the emergency room staff accelerated their two goals — to keep Gary alive while they could locate and administer the antivenin.

As a staff member called nearby Ellen Trout Zoo in search of the drug, Gary's condition became critical. His body swelled, as if he had gained 40 pounds in a matter of minutes, and blood began oozing out of every orifice of his body.

The doctors and nurses knew that most patients who suffer such cataclysmic trauma do not survive.

In a life-saving, if uncanny twist, zoo officials said that they indeed had 10 vials of Canebrake snake antivenin — explaining that the vials had been delivered to the zoo, by nothing more than chance timing, that very morning.

The vials were hurried to the medical center where the liquid inside all of the 10 small vials was injected into Gary.

While that dosage of antivenin bought him and his caregivers a little time, the quantity was not enough to save him. He was placed on a respirator and given a platelet transfusion to counter his excessive bleeding.

That night and through the next day, a small army of people — members of the medical center staff, officials at the zoo, along with individuals from the local poison control center and the Texas Parks and Wildlife Department — desperately searched for more Canebrake antivenin.

"I never realized what a small amount of poison

could do to a person's body," remembers intensive care nurse Phillip Lowery, who with the help of others finally located 40 additional vials of the drug in Houston, about 100 miles away.

Without delay, an emergency runner known as a "Hot Shot" — a very expensive, very fast driver — was hired to speed the vials to Lufkin.

By the time the runner dashed into the medical center, almost 48 hours had passed since Gary had been bitten. His critical condition had worsened — and was quickly deteriorating.

Working with experts at the poison control center, physicians at the medical center decided to inject the full contents of the 40 small vials of antivenin into Gary. The doctors also ordered four units of blood plasma. Then, the medical caregivers could do nothing but wait.

During those first three days, news of Gary's encounter with the rattlesnake and his precarious plight spread throughout eastern Texas.

In his job doing electrical maintenance at area schools, Gary had become a favorite of both teachers and children who could always count on his professional skills and his friendly smile. So as the news covered the countryside, prayers for Gary were plentiful, far beyond those of his family members and close friends.

The fourth day passed with only the slight improvement of weaning Gary off the ventilator so that he could breathe on his own.

Then came the fifth day, Friday, February 24.

"I remember someone asking me if I knew what day it was," Gary says. "I thought I had been out for one night, so I said Tuesday. I was a little surprised when they said it was Friday, but after they explained everything that had gone on the whole week and said how very lucky I had been, I was just glad to be alive."

From that day on, Gary has continued to progress. When he was released from the medical center — 30 pounds lighter than when his wife rushed him there — the only ongoing treatment ordered was lots and lots of rest. Within weeks, Gary regained the strength to return to work, then nine months and several extensive checkups later, his doctors could find no adverse effects from the tortuous trauma his body withstood during those five frightening days.

"I have been blessed," he says, matter-of-factly. "So many people went out of their way to work so hard to help me, folks at the hospital, at the zoo and a lot of people I didn't even know.

"I also believe in prayers now a lot more than I used to. People were praying for me up and down the roads of east Texas and even farther.

"I know I wouldn't have made it without all the help and all the prayers."

When Gary first returned home from the medical center, he asked his brother to release the Canebrake rattler and other snakes he had collected back into the wild.

A few days later, Gary received a call from a state wildlife officer who informed him that several of the snakes were on the endangered species list, a fact that carried a hefty fine and the possibility of arrest for persons who collected them.

"I told the officer we'd already let the snakes go but that I knew he would have to fine me or do whatever he had to," Gary says.

"Since he knew all about the bite and everything I had been through, the officer said he thought I had probably been punished enough, if I had learned my lesson.

"I told him I certainly had learned my lesson about snakes, along with another lesson. The power of prayers."

Sherry Peterson
Columbia Woodland Heights Medical Center
Lufkin, Texas

CAN YOU HELP?

Unlike the masses of medical messages faxed to the busy office of Kathleen Walker Williams at Columbia Alaska Regional Hospital in Anchorage, one instantly caught her eye in early 1996.

"Can You Help?"

That was the simple plea which would soon turn Kathleen into a key link in a long chain of largely happenstance events that would break international barriers of culture, language and distance to give a young man a new chance at life.

"When I first saw the fax, I thought it was pretty strange," says Kathleen, program director for the RehabCare Unit at the hospital. "But it made me curious enough to take it home that night and call the number to find out what it was all about."

It was a tangled story which first began in September 1995 and thousands of miles away on the war-shattered streets of Grozny, the Chechen capital. There, a young man named Dmitri Matveev — an officer in the Russian national police — had been shot while attempting to arrest an arms smuggler. The bullet had sliced through his spinal cord, paralyzing him except for minor movements in his upper body — a condition considered worse than death among most in his native land where rehabilitation therapy is virtually non-existent.

Before the shot was fired, Dmitri had been a strapping, 215-pound weight lifter who was known to go out of his way to help his family, friends and strangers, alike. After two months in a Moscow hospital, Dmitri — 24 years old and a physical shell of his former self — was sent home to spend the rest of his life flat on his back in bed, as helpless as a newborn.

The story would have ended there if fate hadn't decided to flex its muscles.

An orthopedic surgeon for the Alaska Native Medical Center was on a business trip in Dmitri's hometown of Magadan, a four-hour flight from Anchorage across the frigid Bering Sea. While there, someone had handed him a small stack of papers with the words "Can You Help?" written across the top. From the accompanying information, the surgeon learned that Dmitri's childhood friends were attempting to do the impossible — give their friend hope for a better life.

Using a word-of-mouth campaign, their efforts had been so relentless that Dmitri's story had captured the attention of political and business leaders in Magadan. And by chance, the governor of Magadan and an official from the Omolon Gold

Mining Company had travel plans to Anchorage in early 1996.

"It was shortly before their trip that I got the fax," Kathleen says. "What had happened was that the orthopedic surgeon had brought the papers from Magadan back home and then faxed them to us."

Like everyone who had heard about Dmitri, Kathleen and the other staff members at the hospital wanted to help — particularly Dr. Eric Carlsen, medical director of the RehabCare Unit and a quadriplegic from a spinal cord injury during his college years.

"So one day, the Magadan governor and the contact from the mining company came to the hospital and toured our unit," Kathleen explains. "Afterwards, we went into Dr. Carlsen's office and he closed the door. The governor asked straight out if we could make Dmitri walk again. Dr. Carlsen said no. But then he explained that we could give Dmitri as much functional independence as possible and show him how to have a life in a wheelchair. The governor said, 'Fine. We'd like to send him.' And then they left."

Money was collected by Dmitri's friends from individuals and companies for his treatment and forwarded to the Alaska hospital. And with a ticket donated by Russia's Aeroflot Airlines, Dmitri arrived in Anchorage on July 15, 1996.

Kathleen made arrangements that he would be cleared by U.S. Customs agents as quickly as possible.

Then, she saw him for the first time.

"Even though he was in a reclining wheelchair, I could tell he was tall," she says. "He was very thin. His dark hair was very short. And he was so somber looking, no smile at all."

A translator — a student from Magadan studying in Alaska — was provided by the Magadan governor, and the rehabilitation of Dmitri was ready to begin. At first, his progress came in small measures — aided not only by his new "family" of staff members at the hospital, but also caring Anchorage citizens who heard about the young visitor from Russia.

Then, the intense treatment process began.

In addition to physical and occupational therapy, the staff in the unit used their hearts, minds and special skills to help him. By championing the limited mobility he had in his shoulders and arms, Dmitri was fitted with apparatus which allowed him to learn how to feed himself, dress himself and maneuver his wheelchair. Then, Dmitri learned how to move from his wheelchair to his bed and back again, tend to himself in the bathroom, as well as get in and out of a car, on his own power.

Then came the fun things, thanks to the time, effort and donation of special equipment from the hospital staff and others. Dmitri went swimming. He went fishing for world-famous Alaskan salmon. He went on a personally-guided tour of the picture-post-card perfect Alaskan mountains and woods. And he went to a real rodeo, returning with a top-of-the-line cowboy hat given to him by a local retailer.

"We watched Dmitri come back to life," Kathleen says simply.

As the days of his six-week rehabilitation wound down, Dmitri's questions about what type of future family life he could expect were reassured by the beautiful, bubbly, 8-month-old daughter of his lead rehabilitation physician and fellow quadriplegic, Dr. Carlsen.

Fate even had an answer for the fears Dmitri and the hospital staff had for his reintroduction to Russian life once he returned home. A young Catholic priest by the name of Father Mike who had recently moved to Magadan knew helping Dmitri readjust was one of God's callings.

"We all knew the day was coming that we had done everything we could and Dmitri would be going home," Kathleen says. "Those last few days before his mother flew over to take him home, we had all kinds of parties and everyone kept bringing Dmitri gifts. It was wonderful."

Dmitri's wish was to meet his mother at the Anchorage airport. Though the plane was to land at 3 a.m., the woman from U.S. Customs — who had taken the time to learn how to help him transfer from his wheelchair into her car to take him on many sightseeing trips around Anchorage — drove Dmitri to the airport.

The reunion was a monument to miracles — both mother and son wept as Dmitri showed off his new freedom in his wheelchair.

"When I got to the hospital," Kathleen remembers, "his mother walked into my office. Without an interpreter, she gave me a doily she had crocheted and said, 'I love you.' With those three words, I knew what she was trying to say. She wanted to thank me, as well as thank every member of our staff and everyone else along the way who had helped give her son a new opportunity to live a full life.

"It was a very emotional moment."

Dmitri and his mother returned to Magadan on August 26, 1996.

With him, he took a powerful dream of one day

opening a center to help the disabled in his own country.

What he left behind was just as powerful.

"Dmitri crawled into our hearts," Kathleen adds, with happy tears in her eyes. "We still miss him, and a part of us always will. Everything about him was so special."

What Kathleen — along with all the many others who helped the young man from Russia — is still too close to see are the countless wonders which always seem to follow those who say "Yes" whenever asked "Can You Help?"

Larry Andrews
Columbia Alaska Regional Hospital
Anchorage, Alaska

SWOOSH

As sisters, Mary Lois and Myrtle Kervin could hardly have been closer.

With Mary Lois only 16 months older, the two girls were inseparable growing up in the late 1920s in the rich-dirt farmlands of Red Level, Alabama.

Since the only school was miles away and Mary Lois was small for her age, their parents kept Mary Lois at home a year so the girls could enter first grade together. There, they dressed alike, did their homework together, marveled at fairy tales and did most of their dreaming about their future lives together.

And they followed through with those dreams.

After graduating from Red Level High School, they both attended a year-long course at Massey Draughn Business College in Montgomery before moving, together of course, to the friendly town of Andalusia, about halfway between Montgomery and Mobile.

There, Myrtle took a position as a secretary, while Mary Lois went to work as a bookkeeper.

Even after Mary Lois married Perry Beesley in 1950, the two sisters remained as tight as ever. And their relationship was cemented even more several years later with the birth of Mary Allyn, the only child of Perry and Mary Lois.

"They had a big house at the time and Mary Allyn was growing up and getting ready to start school," Myrtle says, adding with a laugh that her sister liked to sleep late in the morning.

"They told me if I would move in, they would fix me an apartment in the house and I could live there, free of charge, if I would take Mary Allyn to school on my way to work in the mornings.

"I was boarding with some teachers across town at the time, and I loved the idea. Of course I insisted on paying my own way, but I was happy to move in with them."

As the decades passed, more expansions were made to the house, giving Myrtle her own "home," including her own carport and private entrance. And as Mary Lois kept the role she loved as a stay-at-home mother, Myrtle climbed the career ladder to become a member of the board as well as secretary-treasurer of Taylor Parts, an automotive parts distributor — the company where she first started out as a secretary.

As the more outgoing of the two sisters, Myrtle kept extremely active in church and civic affairs, being honored time and again for her hard work and dedication, along with coming in fourth at Alabama's

Ms. Senior America contest a few years ago.

Settling into life past their 70-year milestones, the sisters couldn't have asked for a better life or closer relationship. But unlike the fairy tales of their youth, they found themselves living in the real world in the summer of 1995 when Mary Lois fell ill.

After a series of tests, the diagnosis was terminal lung cancer, a cruel double-twist since Mary Lois was never a smoker.

"Of course I knew everything, even that the doctors said they couldn't promise that Mary Lois would be with us past the first of the year," Myrtle says. "But while this might be a little hard to understand, she and I never discussed her illness, not once. I think we both knew that was just something we couldn't do after being together so long.

"I don't think either one of us could have talked about it, at least directly, without both of us falling completely apart."

By late October 1995, their silent support system was at maximum sister strength. Several times a day, Myrtle would open the door in her apartment that led down a long corridor to Mary Lois' bedroom. There, they would talk and laugh as their last days together on Earth counted down.

"We were both very religious," Myrtle says, "but

while I was the type to be more active in the church, teaching Sunday School and such as I do, I always knew Mary Lois had a deeper relationship with the Lord. When it came to her faith, she was as solid as a rock."

Then one morning in mid-November 1995 as Myrtle prepared to walk down the hall to visit Mary Lois, her own religious convictions took on an equally solid turn — in a way that she never could have dreamed, much less imagined.

"I opened the door to the hallway and I saw the most incredible thing, an angel," Myrtle says, her voice still in awe of the experience. "I immediately stopped. I never did look up. I just focused on the skirt. She was wearing a beautiful, long, white gown with a full skirt made of several layers of thin material.

"As I stood there, the material from the skirt wrapped around and around me until I was totally engulfed. Then after a few moments, the material started slowly unwinding, and as it went past my face, I could hear the material making the sounds of 'swoosh ... swoosh ... swoosh' until it disappeared. Then a thick, white cloud rose up from the floor, completely surrounding me.

"Suddenly, I had this wonderful feeling of calmness and total peace before the cloud disappeared. Then I heard a voice behind me say, 'Everything is going to be all right.' I couldn't tell if it was a man or a woman. It wasn't feminine and it wasn't masculine. It was just so peaceful, I wasn't scared or anything, just calm, humbled and grateful."

When the experience ended, Myrtle walked on down the hallway and told her sister what had happened, repeating what the angel had said, "Everything is going to be all right."

The words seemed to soothe Mary Lois as much as Myrtle.

Three days later, a representative from Andalusia's chamber of commerce called and told Myrtle she had been selected, if she would agree, to be the "angel" in the Christmas parade a few weeks away.

Churning with emotion at the coincidence of her recent experience and the invitation, she accepted.

On the Friday night of December 1, 1995, Myrtle — dressed in the flowing white gown of an angel — rode on a float in the Andalusia Christmas Parade.

Less than 24 hours later, on Saturday night December 2, 1995, Myrtle was standing at her sister's beside, rubbing her hand and repeating the angel's promise, when Mary Lois slipped silently and soundly into her final sleep.

Through the early months of 1996, Myrtle —
alone for the first time in her life without Mary Lois —
kept as busy as she could. And then in May, she was
given an opportunity that she knew her sister would
approve — the chance to become one of the charter
members of the National Association of Senior
Friends at Columbia Andalusia Regional Hospital.

"Senior Friends is such a marvelous organiza-
tion," Myrtle says. "It offers those of us who are
seniors a chance to interact with the world, make
new friends and learn new things such as tips on fit-
ness and nutrition.

"And for me, joining Senior Friends couldn't
have come along at a better time in my life."

Today, Myrtle knows the opportunity to meet
new friends — much like her encounter with the
angel — is God's way, perhaps with a little prodding
from her loving sister, to let her know that even in the
darkest grief, "everything will be all right."

Mary Stewart
Columbia Andalusia Regional Hospital
Andalusia, Alabama

MONA'S MASTER PEACE

A certain serenity plays at the corners of her mouth whenever Mona Freshour starts to smile, a look not unlike the mysterious smile of Mona Lisa captured by Leonardo da Vinci's master brushstrokes centuries ago.

But in modern-day life, Mona Freshour has proven that she has much more to offer than just a smiling face.

"Mona has such a positive, spiritual attitude about her," says the Rev. Andrew Gerns, director of pastoral care at St. Joseph's Hospital in the Ohio River Valley town of Parkersburg, West Virginia.

"She's jovial, warm-hearted and open. She takes time for people, and she brings a sort of peacefulness to everyone she meets."

Perhaps the most special thing of all about Mona is that her serenity, playfulness and peacefulness was not shaken in March 1996 when she was diagnosed with a rare form of esophageal cancer — and given only several months to live.

"Wouldn't you know it," Mona says with a laugh, "here I go and get a cancer that's almost always found in 70-year-old men who smoked and drank most of their lives.

"And here I am a single, 40-year-old woman, who's never smoked or drank. Go figure!"

Despite the fact that Mona has out-lived her doctors' first prediction of longevity with the disease, she is still in a heated battle with the cancer. After surgery in April and chemotherapy treatments through the summer, she is slated for yet another round of surgeries and treatments through the fall and winter of 1996.

Yet her uplifting attitude is boundless.

The fact is, it has spilled over to the staff at St. Joseph's where Mona, a nurse — who happens to have been blessed with a spine-tingling singing voice — works as the administrative assistant to the chief nursing officer.

"It is amazing," Rev. Gerns says. "Mona has always been a very special person to all of us, but the way she has handled her illness with both a positive attitude and unyielding faith has been the catalyst for a true spiritual revolution here at the hospital.

"Other people have begun to take personal reflections of themselves as they've watched Mona through all these months. You see, Mona isn't the kind of person who reserves her faith for Sunday mornings.

"She lives it every day, and she has a dual attitude about her illness. First, she is completely confident that she will be cured. Second, at the very same time, she's comfortable with the fact that if things don't work out, that will be okay, too.

"A lot of people, myself included, have been impressed seeing her deal with cancer like that. And it has made a difference to us all."

The first outward sign of the "revolution" at St. Joseph's came on April 8, 1996 when Mona underwent surgery.

Instead of the usual routine of giving a dollar for flowers or a fruit basket, the St. Joseph's staff — with absolutely no prodding from Rev. Gerns or his four chaplains in the pastoral care office — took it upon themselves to hold a prayer vigil in the hospital chapel while Mona was in surgery in New York.

"They asked me to organize it," Rev. Gerns says, with obvious wonder still touching his words.

"Their idea was simple. They would have people volunteer to be in the chapel in 15-minute intervals from 6:30 a.m. until noon to pray for Mona during the time of her scheduled operation. Anyone could come at any time, but they wanted to make sure someone was there all the time, so the staff chaplains and I agreed to fill in when there were blank spaces on the list.

"It's hard to explain how much their idea for the prayer vigil meant to me. It's the type of thing that people in my profession hope for all the time but only rarely encounter, people coming to us to organize acts of faith they have decided to do themselves."

As far as the anticipated "blank spaces" on the

prayer vigil list was concerned, no one should have worried.

The response was phenomenal.

Dozens of staff members flooded the chapel, foregoing their normal morning breaks to pray for Mona. Then at 11:30 a.m., Rev. Gerns, overwhelmed by the response, conducted a 30-minute prayer and communion service to conclude the vigil — one of the best-attended services in his memory at St. Joseph's.

Walking out of the chapel, he knew what the staff had experienced throughout the morning was too good to keep from Mona, herself. Scrambling through several telephone calls, he finally dialed the number at the hospital.

A young woman, a Rabbinical student, answered the phone, and Rev. Gerns explained the whole story, asking her to please convey the message as soon as Mona awakened from surgery.

"It was about 7 p.m. when I woke up in the recovery room and this young woman was there, telling me about the all-morning prayer vigil my friends at St. Joseph's had for me," Mona says, with her appreciative, trademark smile.

"It meant everything to me. I told her to call them back, tell everyone I loved them and that I'd be home soon."

True to her word, Mona was soon back in West Virginia, preparing for a summer of chemotherapy, when she, herself, got caught up in what she calls the "spiritual awakening" at St. Joseph's.

"I realized that one reason I might be walking this journey is that God wants me to touch others," she says. "I've always known we are all here for a purpose, all in His time and in His keeping.

"Now, being able to talk to patients who have been newly diagnosed with cancer, I have a new understanding of what to tell them since I am living with cancer, too.

"The main thing I say is this. Cancer will not control my life. I will control the cancer. And when the time comes, when I have learned what God wants me to learn on this journey, He will lift me out of here."

For now, Mona is back to singing once again, as she plans for the additional surgeries and treatments through late 1996.

When asked how she maintains her "sweet serenity," she doesn't hesitate to give credit to her parents, her brother David and his family, her close friends — along with "my very, very strong relationship with Christ."

"But don't get the idea I'm not human," she says, both sincerely and teasingly. "I'm human and there are fearful times, but fortunately those times don't last for me.

"And looking at it another way, the cancer has done lots of positive things for me.

"First, it slammed me into perspective, immediately, helping me to prioritize what's important and what's not.

"It's also taught me how to live a day at a time because I can't do anything about tomorrow. That's a lesson that has helped me every day since I've been back at work, sharing that message with new cancer patients."

Of her own fate, Mona smiles as she adds:

"Well, it's like this. My own prayer is that my family and friends here and my God in Heaven will be proud of me for the way I handled this sort of scary thing. But the bigger news, of course, is that God has a plan for all of us.

"So I just figure that I'm lucky to have been here, and whenever God is ready to take me out of this situation, I'm ready.

"But, at least for today, I'm ready to stay."

Sue Sowards
St. Joseph's Hospital in affiliation with Columbia
Parkersburg, West Virginia

MIRACLES IN OUR MIDST

Stories of Life, Love, Kindness And Other Miracles

IS AVAILABLE
AT MANY COLUMBIA FACILITIES
TO ORDER ADDITIONAL COPIES
PLEASE CALL

1-800-COLUMBIA

(Shipping and handling charges
will be added to all telephone orders)